FASHION
EMBROIDERY

FASHION EMBROIDERY

EMBROIDERY TECHNIQUES AND INSPIRATION
FOR HAUTE-COUTURE CLOTHING

JESSICA JANE PILE

BATSFORD

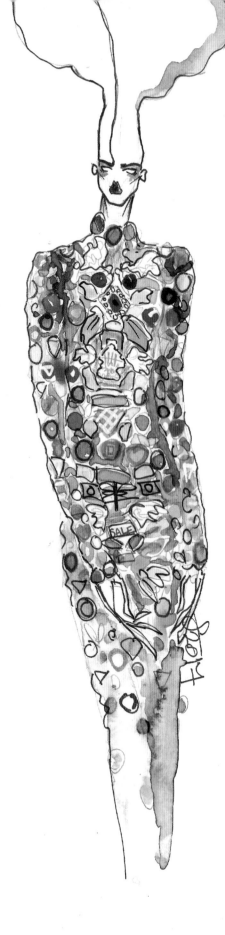

MIX
Paper from
responsible sources
FSC® C104723

FIRST PUBLISHED IN THE UNITED KINGDOM IN 2018 BY BATSFORD

43 GREAT ORMOND STREET

LONDON WC1N 3HZ

AN IMPRINT OF PAVILION BOOKS COMPANY LTD

COPYRIGHT © BATSFORD, 2018

TEXT COPYRIGHT © JESSICA JANE PILE, 2018

ISBN: 9781849944748

A CIP CATALOGUE RECORD FOR THIS BOOK IS AVAILABLE FROM
THE BRITISH LIBRARY.

25 24 23 22 21 20 19

10 9 8 7 6 5 4 3

REPRODUCTION BY MISSION, HONG KONG

PRINTED BY TOPPAN LEEFUNG PRINTING LTD, CHINA

THIS BOOK CAN BE ORDERED DIRECT FROM THE PUBLISHER AT THE
WEBSITE WWW.PAVILIONBOOKS.COM, OR TRY YOUR LOCAL BOOKSHOP.

DISTRIBUTED IN THE UNITED STATES AND CANADA BY
STERLING PUBLISHING CO., INC. 1166 AVENUE OF THE AMERICAS,
17TH FLOOR, NEW YORK, NY 10036

CONTENTS

◀ Oscar de la Renta
(Autumn/Winter, 2013).
Hand-beaded dress with
ribbon detailing.

INTRODUCTION

It is hard for me to think about fashion and not consider embroidery as one of its defining features. During every fashion week I search the catwalk shows for the slightest glimmer of embroidery. Obviously, there are the embroidery regulars like Elie Saab and Valentino, whose shows you only need to watch for a few seconds before the embroidery becomes immediately noticeable, but there are others where you have to look more closely. As with any modern style, it might appear that embroidery comes in and out of fashion, like the little black dress, but, if you look closely, you will realize that in fact embroidery is there all the time. It is often used to create patterns and yet give the impression that it is not really embroidery at all. This is what I love about it — it is versatile and sometimes hard to see, but it is there, coming down the runway more often that Kate Moss.

In this book, I will look at embroidery in all aspects of fashion, be it haute couture, luxury or high-street fashion. You will learn about the history of fashion and embroidery, and I will teach you the basics of the hand-embroidery techniques used by the high-end fashion houses, as well as how to create your own embroidery designs.

 Jenny Packham (Autumn/Winter, 2016).
Tambour-beaded floral detail in sequins.

◤ Elie Saab Haute Couture (Autumn/Winter, 2016).
Three-dimensional embroidered birds and flowers
with feathers and sequins.

EMBROIDERY IN FASHION

MACHINE VERSUS HAND EMBROIDERY

We have recently seen a great resurgence of embroidery in fashion. It has not only graced almost every garment sent down the haute-couture and ready-to-wear runways during recent shows, but it has also been added to a huge number of items in high-street stores. From floral patterns on tulle dresses and fashion patches covering any wearable piece to personalising your garment with your own name, embroidery has really shown its diversity. Personalisation has become hugely popular following the recession of 2008. Whether this involves personalising with patching or monogramming, this idea has been used by almost every brand: Burberry offer a personalisation service that allows you to add embroidered initials to your backpack or poncho, while Gucci gives customers the option to choose different embroidery patches to attach to their chosen jacket. Embroidery has filtered into every aspect of fashion and it has been wonderful to see.

I like to separate the fashion industry into three categories: haute couture, ready-to-wear and high street. Manufacturers in each of these markets use embroidery in different ways. The haute-couture houses will always use hand embroidery; ready-to-wear will use a mixture of hand embroidery, hand-guided machine embroidery and machine embroidery; high-street fashion will mainly use machine embroidery. Factors such as sustainability, cost and the target market will determine the type of embroidery used and within which market.

These factors are common to any industry and define the standards of quality that we expect when investing money in a purchase. Hand embroidery is expensive: it takes time and dedication to achieve the highest level of skill; the embroiderers have often trained for 4–5 years before they are able to work on a sellable garment. The techniques are unique and have been used for centuries, and the equipment used in embroidery ateliers around the world also remains unchanged. The techniques of hand embroidery can rarely be entirely replicated by machine, which is why hand embroidery is still widely used in high-end fashion.

The invention of machine embroidery has, however, allowed the high-street brands to mimic hand embroidery. Although machine embroidery cannot achieve the artistry of hand embroidery, machines have allowed embroidery to fit into the ever-growing fast fashion industry. Many people are unable to tell the difference between hand embroidery and machine embroidery, and people often ask me how it is possible to distinguish between the two. It is a fair question. Most people have had very little exposure to hand embroidery and it is easy to assume that technology has created a faster, more cost-effective way of creating embroidery, which can support the fickle consumers of today's disposable fashion. Fortunately, the haute-couture and luxury industries still support the craft of hand embroidery. Having said that, embroidery is still embroidery, whether it is done by machine or by hand, and although machines cannot always replicate hand embroidery, each shines in different ways. It is an alternative rather than a replacement. Although this book will only teach you how do hand embroidery in fashion, I hope by reading and learning to stitch you will come to identify the difference between the two and appreciate embroidery of all types.

▶ Dolce & Gabbana (Spring/Summer, 2016) uses a mixture of hand beading and hand-guided embroidery to personalise their collection.

A BRIEF HISTORY OF FASHION EMBROIDERY

The earliest form of hand embroidery is still a matter of debate. One theory is that it may have come from the Middle East and dates back to the 3rd century AD. However, another theory states it can be dated back to as early as 1300BC and appears on clothing found in Tutankhamun's coffin. The first of these is officially documented as the earliest form of embroidery, while the latter is still being researched. Both of these predate the invention of 'fashion design' as we know it by over 1,500 years. The embroidery at either date uses beading and thread stitching on linen bases, similar to the embroidery techniques used today. Painted vases and sculptures have been useful to identify embroidery as they depict figures from various ancient civilisations wearing embroidered garments.

One of the oldest pieces of embroidery still in existence is the Bayeux Tapestry that dates from the 1070s. Although called a 'tapestry' it is actually a piece of embroidery. It took approximately ten years to complete, and is over 70m (230ft) long. Made in England the embroidery depicts events leading up to the Battle of Hastings. It is named the 'Bayeux' Tapestry as the earliest record of the embroidery is in the cathedral at Bayeux, where it is still housed today.

Embroidery flourished in England during the 13th–15th centuries with the birth of a new style called *Opus Anglicanum* that was often used in ecclesiastical hangings. The style comprised two types of stitches, split stitch and underside couching, and used metal and cotton threads to create incredibly detailed embroidery. It was such a time-consuming technique that the embroidery of this era became extremely sought after, and pieces were presented as diplomatic gifts. Examples of *Opus Anglicanum* that have survived to the present day are prized possessions.

By the 17th century embroidery had gained in popularity and the use of beads and pearls could be seen in lavishly embroidered garments and furnishings. Embroidery was used as a sign of social status and women would create samplers as a sign of their position and wealth. In a similar way during this era military embroidery showed a soldier's rank as it was used on military badges and accoutrements. It is still used in this way today.

In the 19th century the term haute couture was coined by Charles Frederick Worth. Translated from French it means 'high sewing', and represents the beginning of fashion as we know it today. Worth was

▲ Military badges embroidered by Hand & Lock.

◀ Macson uses military-inspired badges in its latest collection.

◀◀ The Bayeux Tapestry is one of the earliest pieces of embroidery still in existence. One theory is that it was made in the 1070s by Queen Matilda, the wife of William I, as shown here.

the founder of the House of Worth, which was established in 1858. Worth modernized 19th-century dresses by taking the traditional style and creating more wearable, everyday outfits. He is considered to have revolutionised the fashion industry, making his garments the most sought-after pieces of their time. Worth was able to give his clients the opportunity to choose each component of their outfit, from the finest fabric, to the most delicate embroidery, and even the style of the buttons. It was a truly unique experience that had not existed before.

Today in France the term 'haute couture' is protected by law and can only be used by companies who meet specific, well-defined standards. These standards are set out by the *Fedération de la Haute Couture et de la Mode* – the governing body of the French fashion industry, which in turn grew out of a grouping founded by Charles Frederick Worth. The strict requirements state that the house must have a full-time workshop that employs no fewer than 20 staff members; they must be based in Paris and must offer a 'made-to-measure' service with personal fittings; and finally they must present two collections a year that include daytime, formal and evening wear that are presented in January and July.

Haute couture is an expensive business. The use of high-quality fabric and delicate embroidery can mean that some pieces will take up to 700 hours to complete and cost in excess of £8,000. Household names that still operate in the business are Chanel, Elie Saab, Christian Dior, Valentino and Jean-Paul Gaultier.

The modern embroidery and fashion industry is global. The development of sewing and embroidery machines has enabled the mass production of garments, often in third-world countries to save costs. Because of consumer demand for fast fashion, the high street was born, with retailers like Biba, Topshop and Zara allowing the customer to keep up with fashion trends at affordable prices.

Today the love affair with embroidery and fashion is still strong, whether it is through painstakingly detailed hand embroidery, or a small pieces of machine embroidery on a denim jacket. Embroidery may have been around for over 1,500 years before fashion design as we know it was invented, but it is hard not to associate the two.

◄ Chanel (Spring/Summer, 2015), one of the few fashion houses still operating in the haute-couture business.

▲ The English fashion designer Charles Frederick Worth revolutionised the fashion industry and coined the term 'haute couture'.

THE FINER DETAILS

Knowing how to identify the different types of embroidery is something that comes with experience. It is often difficult to look at a piece of embroidery on a garment and know how it is embroidered. I generally find the best place to start is by looking at the back of the embroidery; this will usually tell you whether it has been embroidered by hand or machine. Once you have determined this you will then be able to look at the stitch of the embroidery to understand what techniques have been used.

There are so many different techniques in embroidery that it is difficult to know and identify them all, but if you have a good enough knowledge about embroidery and are able to break down the stitches, you will be able to work out how a particular piece has been done. While writing this book I have discovered techniques I had not previously been aware of, seen how traditional techniques have been altered or developed and also how unusual materials have been used in embroidery.

MACHINE EMBROIDERY

Machine embroidery is always quite easy to recognize if are able to look at the back of the embroidery. Machine embroidery is always produced with a backing material to support the work while in the frame. If you are able to see a material that looks similar to paper around the edge of the stitching you will be looking at a piece of machine embroidery.

A stitch called a tajima stitch is used to fill larger areas of machine embroidery. Here the stitches create a brick formation across the area and the stitches are all exactly the same size. Smaller areas will be embroidered in a satin stitch that looks exactly like a hand-embroidered stitch from the front, but, if you look at the back, you will be able to see the bobbin thread. Machine embroidery is created using a digital computer programme where the embroidery stitches are selected, and areas are completed in sections rather than with individual stitches. To fill an area the machine is only able to use one needle at a time; as a result it is difficult to blend two colours together and the embroidery tends to have a blocky look. As already mentioned above, the final telltale sign of machine embroidery is the bobbin thread: any embroidery done with a machine will have a bobbin thread that keeps the top stitching in place.

▲ Machine-embroidered patches by Hand & Lock (Autumn/Winter, 2016). Areas of stitch are completed in sections using a digital computer programme.

▶ Machine-embroidered jacket by Prada (Autumn/Winter, 2016).

▶ This piece of embroidery uses mainly satin stitches. You can see how the colours do not blend together, indicating that it was made by machine.

◀ Nguyen Cong Tri uses a mixture of machine embroidery and hand embroidery to create these 3D embroidered pieces. Central sections of the flowers are beaded, while the outer borders are machine embroidered. Detail in the petals is hand-embroidered – notice the way the two colours blend.

▲ Mary Katrantzou was mainly known for print until her Autumn/Winter 2014 show in which every piece in her collection was covered in embroidery. This piece (above, and detail above left) was embroidered by Hand & Lock. It is machine embroidered on the base and then worked into with beads, sequins, goldwork and silk shading.

IRISH AND CORNELY MACHINES

I have not mentioned Irish and Cornely machines thus far, but they do play a relatively large role in the embroidery and fashion world.

IRISH MACHINE: Also known as a freehand embroidery machine, this creates a satin stitch, long and short stitches, and zigzag stitches. It is similar to the digital machine, where the formation of the stitches is the same, however, as the Irish machine is controlled by a person guiding the fabric underneath, it produces much more fluid stitches. In addition, because of the freedom you have to move the needle around your fabric you are able to blend colours as you would in hand embroidery, and this will give much more depth to the embroidery than machine embroidery. Again, the embroidery will always have the telltale bobbin thread on the back. The benefit to hand-guided machine embroidery is that you are able to work on much larger areas, whereas, on a digital machine you are limited by the size of frame.

CORNELY MACHINE: This is also a hand-guided machine where the fabric is guided under the needle to produce the pattern. The Cornely machine produces a chain stitch that is exactly the same as that used for tambour beading. In fact, it is very difficult to tell the difference between hand-tamboured chain stitch and a chain stitch from the Cornely machine. Both feed the thread from underneath and the Cornely, unlike other machines, does not have a bobbin thread. The giveaway for me is the consistency of the size of stitches: a Cornely machine is fixed at a set stitch size that means that the embroidery will be totally consistent in a line of stitches. Even the most experienced embroiderer would struggle to make their stitches as consistent as the Cornely machine.

▲ This is a piece being stitched in an Irish embroidery machine; as you can see, the machine allows free movement and blending of the colours.

▶ Hand-guided embroidery using the Irish machine decorates a bright bag to spectacular effect. The blended colours achieve greater depth than is possible with standard machine embroidery.

23

◀ Hand & Lock Collection (Spring/Summer, 2016)
Here you can see that the Irish machine has been
used to outline areas with satin stitch. Negative
spaces can then be cut away, giving the appearance
of lace.

▶ Naeem Khan (Spring/Summer, 2016) uses the
Cornely embroidery machine to create detailed
embroidery patterns.

HAND EMBROIDERY

Hand embroidery is quite easy to recognize. Once you have ruled out the possibility of machine embroidery you are only left with hand embroidery. Looking at the materials used in the embroidery is also a telltale sign: hand embroidery can use a huge variety of threads, from thick chenille to thin silk floss. The use of beads and sequins is also an indicator of hand embroidery, although admittedly there are now machines that can attach beads. However, look for usual shapes or large beads, rather than smaller beads sewn in continuous lines.

Hand embroidery is such a vast subject that even if you know a piece is hand embroidered you may not be able to identify all the stitches. Traditional stitches form the basis of embroidery, but each embroiderer may interpret, alter and develop stitches to suit the project. Embroidery in fashion is a prime example of how this can happen: each designer will want to create a style that is on the cutting edge of the new fashion trends. To carry this off the embroiderer will change, develop and alter traditional stitches to create wonderful new and contemporary effects. In this case, instead of trying to identify how something has been done, sometimes it is good just to stand back and appreciate the overall effect of the embroidery.

▶ Ralph & Russo (Spring/Summer, 2017). The beads used here are either crossed-back or clasped. These types of beads can only be hand-embroidered.

▶ Designed by Renée Lindell and embroidered by Hand & Lock, the embroidery shown here uses a variety of materials and samples. The flowers are embroidered in chenille and silk floss threads – these threads are too thick or delicate for machine work. Goldwork materials are also used.

▼ The continuous line of sequins or beads shows that this embroidery by Hand & Lock will have been hand-beaded: there are slight variations in the stitch sizes implying that it has not been done by machine. Larger clasp-back beads have been used, which will have also been attached by hand.

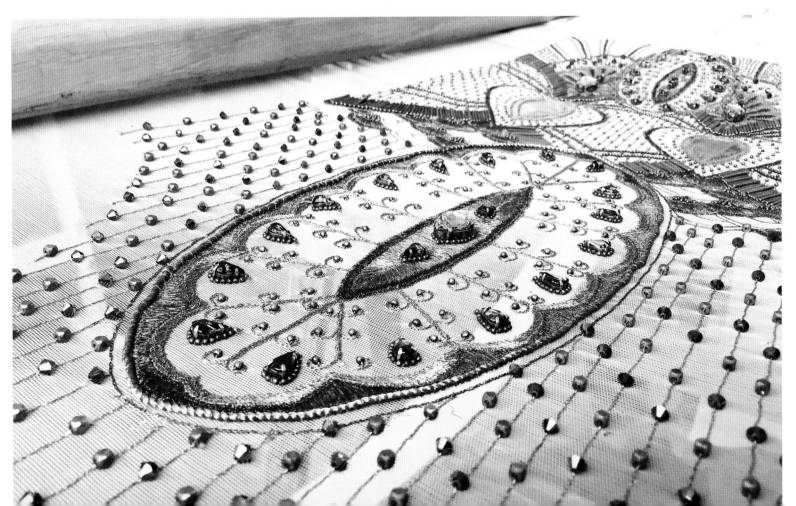

Balmain is known for encrusting garments in embroidery. This piece from the Autumn/Winter 2016 collection is hand- and tambour-beaded with gold circular beads.

Alexander McQueen is always pushing the boundaries of embroidery. This piece from the Autumn/Winter 2012 collection shows the use of tulle that has been gathered, frayed and folded, and then stitched down with beads in-between the folds and gathers.

Another example of Alexander McQueen, this time from the Spring/Summer 2017 collection. The use of materials and techniques is extensive. The small white flowers are comprised of individual white sequins held together in the centre by a cluster of larger yellow beads. The branches and leaves have been hand-embroidered in silk threads. The larger flowers have been embroidered in a variety of beads and sequins in different sizes and shapes. Entire garments in this collection will have been hand-embroidered.

DO IT YOURSELF

CHOOSING THE RIGHT EMBROIDERY FOR YOU

Before starting to learn how to stitch, it is worth taking some time to choose the correct embroidery for you and your project. You will want to approach the project with a perspective of how the embroidery will look on your garment. Here are some helpful tips to bear in mind when deciding where to place the embroidery.

TIPS

- The type of embroidery you choose will depend on where you want to place it. For instance, goldwork embroidery does not fare well on areas that are likely to be creased or on garments that will be exposed to damp. It is advisable not to place goldwork on raincoats or place the embroidery on an elbow or knee because it will break the embroidery.

- All embroidery is quite delicate. Avoid placing embroidery on areas where there could be rubbing or contact. Common areas where this occurs includes under the arms, on the back and in-between the legs.

- If you decide to use beads be aware of where you are placing large beads. Beads will protrude from the surface of the fabric and sometimes have irregular shapes. Bear in mind that beads will rub against the skin or other sections of clothing. Again, placing beads under the arm or in-between the legs will be uncomfortable for the wearer and can often cause more damage to the garment.

- It is always advisable to do embroidery on flat pieces of fabric prior to the garment being made. Embroidery needs tension, so if you have a ready-made garment it will be difficult to embroider onto if you cannot get the section your are embroidering to lie flat without any fabric behind it.

- If you are embroidering close to the edge of flat pattern pieces you will want to make sure that the pattern pieces have been fitted properly to the wearer. Once you place the embroidery on the garment you will not be able to move it. If the embroidery is close to a seam the garment cannot then be taken in.

- When drawing your embroidery design onto your pattern pieces, don't forget seam allowances. As above, if you end up embroidering into the seam allowance, you will not be able to move the embroidery.

- Be aware of the drape of a fabric and how the embroidery will change the drape. Heavy embroidery will pull the fabric down and alter the way it was intended to drape.

- If your garment is pleated or gathered, make sure the position of the embroidery is visible on the pleats or gathers. Also, be aware that dense embroidery will flatten out fabric so therefore you will not be able to bend the fabric on the pleats if it has been placed incorrectly.

Oscar de la Renta (Autumn/Winter, 2014). Choosing the right embroidery for the garment and thinking carefully about its placement and suitability is essential.

GETTING STARTED

When approaching your embroidery design, it is important to remember that your preparation is just as important as your stitching time. Don't underestimate how long you will spend setting up your frame and preparing your fabric. Here is the equipment you will need.

FRAMES

All embroidery will be worked on an embroidery frame of some description: the frame will keep your embroidery tight and prevent it from puckering when removed. The type of frame to choose will depend on the size of the embroidery. There are two main types of frames to work on, a hoop frame and a slate frame.

If you would like to add some embroidery to a garment you already own you will need to use the same frames but with some additional steps. Please note that you cannot embroider onto sleeves or trouser legs without opening the inside seam. If your garment has a lining you will need to open this up to get to the section you would like to embroider. It is also important to bear in mind that the area you want to embroider will need to lie flat on the frame; if you are unable to do this the embroidery will not be possible. See Framing up a garment, page 49, for more instructions.

HOOP FRAME: A hoop frame is a good choice for small embroideries and is easy to assemble. I would always recommend attaching a hoop frame to a stand as this allows you to have both hands free to work. You can get stands that attach to a table or seat stands that are designed so you can stitch while seated. My personal preference when working on a hoop frame is to use a seat stand.

SLATE FRAME: A slate frame is usually the type used by professionals. It allows you to frame large pieces of fabric. It is more complicated to set up than a hoop frame and so it will take longer before you can start stitching. A state frame is generally used when completing longer-term projects as it will maintain the tension over an extended period of time. See pages 44–45 for instructions.

NEEDLES

Choosing the correct needle is very important. There are hundreds of different types of needle on the market that serve all sorts of different functions, so it can sometimes be confusing. With embroidery you should try to keep your needle as small as possible. The smaller your needle, the better definition you will achieve in your embroidery, and the needle will also be less likely to damage the base fabric. A good way to choose the correct needle is by looking at your thread: if you are using a thin thread you can use a small needle; thicker threads require larger needles. The most common size of needle I use for embroidery is a 10 or a 12; other needles I find useful are curved needles, beading needles, chenille needles and a bracing needle for framing.

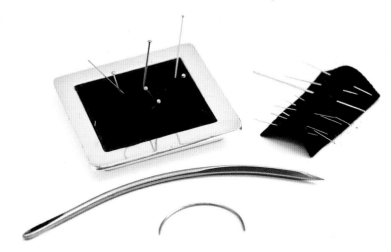

THREADS

Once again there is a huge variety of embroidery threads available, but it is always good to know what you prefer. I use Anchor Stranded Cotton for detailed threadwork, a Gütermann polyester thread for goldwork and a waxed linen thread for tambour beading. Other options are chenille threads, floss threads and metal-foiled threads, such as purl thread or bullion.

MELLOR

This tool is used mainly in goldwork (see page 76) to ease down your bullion into the correct position and to stop it from cracking. It can also be used in other types of embroidery to guide threads into specific positions or stop them from knotting.

SCISSORS

It is important to have a pair of sharp, good-quality scissors. You will need to cut your threads as finely and cleanly as possible to thread your needle, but also to cut away threads from the back of the embroidery.

OTHER USEFUL EQUIPMENT

Tape measure

Mechanical pencil

Pins

Thimble

Wax (for waxing thread)

Pin or needle and cork (for pricking your design)

Rolled up felt (for pouncing your design)

Pencil or disappearing fabric pen

Pounce powder (for transferring patterns to fabric)

Tracing paper (for your design)

Bondaweb or similar (to stiffen fabric)

PREPARING YOUR DESIGN

I started in my career as an embroidery designer, and so consequently I know how important a clear design is to ensure you execute your embroidery properly. As an embroidery designer, your job is to make sure the embroiderer understands how you want the embroidery to look. You need to be able to communicate through the annotation of the design every tiny detail, from the stitch direction and how high you would like the padding, to how many beads you would like within a certain area. If you miss out a single instruction you run the risk of the embroidery looking completely different to what you originally intended. Embroidery can't be unpicked, and trust me I have learned the hard way!

In large embroidery ateliers, there will be a number of designers whose job it is to visualize how they would like the final embroidery to look. This can sometimes be difficult when the only references you have to use are design interpretations and the raw materials. In large haute-couture fashion houses, you will also have the garment designers. They will create a visual design of the whole garment, from here the embroidery designer will come in and interpret from that design how to execute the embroidery.

The embroidery designers will annotate the design with a series of acronyms and abbreviations to reference the materials, colour, size and height. You may have two or three versions of the same design

to clearly communicate to the embroiderer your visual image. How you design the embroidery can also vary based on what techniques you are using – obviously designing embroidery for tambour beading will be different to that for goldwork. Once the embroidery design is handed over to the embroiderer there may be no further communication between the embroiderer and the designer. The embroiderer will interpret the design as precisely as possible through the annotations to create the final embroidered piece.

Embroidery design in fashion is a very small part of the overall look of a garment, but it is hugely important. The overall look of the garment will be reliant on the textures and patterns created by the embroidery. As an embroidery designer you need to be able to focus on the smallest parts of a design but also be able to see the visual effect of the whole piece.

Even if you are designing and executing the embroidery yourself, it is always good to plan your embroidery design before stitching. Embroidery takes a long time, so by the time you get to the final stages, you might have forgotten what you originally intended! I have tried to provide some helpful tips and directions to help you on your design journey.

Once you have all your design prepared you are ready to start transferring your design onto your fabric.

▶ Ralph & Russo (Spring/Summer, 2016). The embroiderer interprets the design from the designer's annotations – every tiny detail contributes to the visual effect of the whole piece.

LINE DRAWING

First of all, you will want to begin with a basic line drawing that will show your outside line and the lines that will separate each area of different stitching. You may also want to include any detailing lines.

MATERIAL/STITCH PLAN

Once you have your line drawing you will want to make a copy so you can work on your material plan. This plan will help you decide what materials you want and also what techniques you might like to use.

1   Look at the sections that you have created within your line drawing and think about the techniques you would like to place in each section; you can use annotation to mark these down. You may also want to mark out your stitch directions.

2   Once you have decided on the techniques you are going to use you can decide on the materials; this could be beads and sequins, or the height or type of thread.

TIP

Make sure all of your outside lines are continuous and do not end randomly. When you are stitching, you will want to fill entire areas, so it is important to create areas that are complete.

Key:
- **A** 1-2 mm of padding
- **B** 2-3 mm of padding
- **C** 3-4 mm of padding

French knots

Pearl purl

Silk shading (long and short stitches)

Satin stitch

Satin stitch **A**

Satin stitch **B**

Satin stitch **B**

Cutwork **C**

All stems in stem stitch

Pearl purl

Leaf stitch

French knots

French knots

Silk shading (long and short stitches)

Cutwork **C**

Leaf stitch

Satin stitch **B**

Cutwork **C**

Silk shading (long and short stitches)

Satin stitch

Satin stitch

COLOUR PLAN

You will also want to work on a third copy of your line drawing showing the colours. Your colour plan will help you to decide whether you would like areas shaded or just block coloured. When designing a colour for beading I find it useful to number my different coloured beads so the plan will essentially be a 'paint by numbers' plan.

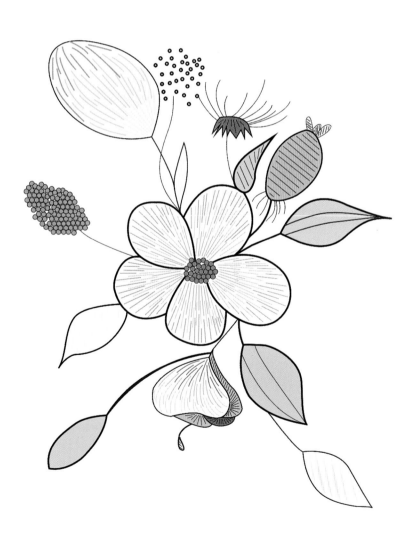

TIPS

• You will need to bear in mind what your base fabric is. Depending on the techniques you are using, the embroidery may change the drape of your fabric or it could be too heavy for the fabric and end up tearing it.

• When deciding on the height of the embroidery I will label different sections by number, with 1 as the lowest height, and 5 as the greatest. I will then create a key at the side for the measurements.

• When using beads, I sometimes find it useful to lay the beads over my design to see if they will fit in smaller or more awkward places. You can also draw round the beads on the design if this is helpful.

TRANSFERRING YOUR DESIGN

Opinion among embroidery professionals varies over whether you should transfer your design onto your fabric prior to framing up or afterwards. I prefer to transfer my design prior to framing as it allows me to move the fabric around without the frame in the way. However, I feel this is down to personal preference, so try both and see which you prefer.

EQUIPMENT

Pricker tool, pin or needle and cork

Rolled-up felt

Pencil or disappearing fabric pen

Pounce powder

Magic tape

TIP

Pounce powder can be bought from most haberdasheries if you do not want to make it yourself (see step 5).

PRICKING AND POUNCING

There are a few different ways to transfer your design onto fabric; I find the most effective and easiest way for most fabrics is pricking and pouncing. You can use this technique for most fabrics apart from netting.

1   First take your line drawing. You will want to transfer this onto tracing paper; you can either print onto tracing paper or you can re-trace your design. Make sure you keep your original design safe, as you will need to refer back to this later.

2   Prick small holes along the lines of your design with a pricker tool, pin or needle, probably 2–4mm apart. If you are embroidering text or a design that is not symmetrical you will want to prick the holes from the back of your design. This will ensure that at the stage of transferring your design your text will read the correct way on the fabric. **A**

3   Once you have pricked your design, you are then ready to transfer this onto your fabric. Place your pricked design onto your fabric in the chosen position with the rough side up (the opposite side to the one you have pricked from).

4   Secure the design in place using tape or weights; for large designs you may want to tack the tracing paper to the fabric for extra security.

5   Once you have your placement, you are ready to transfer the design, a technique otherwise known as pouncing. You do this by using a pounce powder. This can be made from white chalk powder mixed with charcoal powder. By mixing both the white and the black powders together you can create different shades for light and dark fabric. For darker base fabrics you will want a whiter mix; for lighter colours you need a grey.

A

TIP

You can buy professional prickers from any haberdashery, but they may not be as sharp or have as fine a point as a small sewing needle. You can make your own by taking a small needle and pushing the top end into a cork; this will give you a comfortable handle to prick with.

6 Once you have the most appropriate coloured pounce for your base fabric, dab a rolled-up piece of craft felt into the powder – not too much, but enough to lightly show the design.

Work the powder into the pricked design by gently rubbing in a small clockwise motion over the design so the powder drops through the small holes onto the fabric. Remember to keep the design firmly in place. A few clockwise movements will transfer your design effectively. If this does not work first time, do not worry as you can brush the powder away with a cloth brush and start again. **C**

7 Once you feel that enough powder has fallen through the holes of the tracing paper, you can slowly remove the weights or tape and lift the tracing paper up vertically. You will see your design has been safely transferred onto your fabric. You will now need to secure the design onto the fabric as the pounce powder is only temporary and will be wiped away once you start working.

8 To secure the design you will need to draw your design directly onto the fabric using the pounce powder as your guide; use either a sharpened pencil or a disappearing fabric pen to do this. **D** Once this is done you can turn your fabric over and tap the back, knocking away any excess pounce powder. If there is any left after this you can remove it using magic tape.

9 Once your design has been transferred onto the fabric you can either frame up your fabric or start stitching.

TIP

If you are right handed, start drawing from the left and draw across to the right, if you are left handed, start from the right. This will make sure you hand does not wipe away the pounce powder while you are drawing and before you have finished tracing it out.

SETTING UP YOUR FRAME

As mentioned above there are two different types of frame: hoop frames and slate frames. Each needs to be set up in a particular way; here's how to do it.

HOOP FRAME

1 Separate the two hoops from one another and place the central frame on a flat surface. Place your fabric over the central frame so your design is in the centre, well within the hoop.

2 Take your outer hoop and twist the screw on the side to open it. Do not loosen this too much as it will not hold the fabric tight over the central hoop. You can place the outer hoop over the central hoop to check – if the outer hoop just drops easily over the central hoop it is too loose.

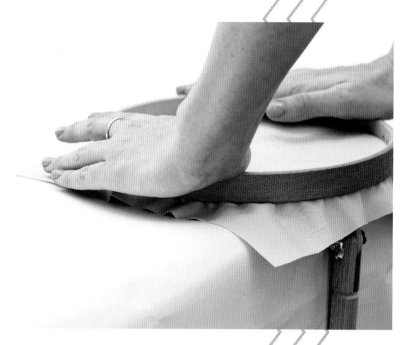

3 Place the outer frame over the fabric and the central hoop, then lean on the outer hoop. You many need to put all your weight onto the outer frame to make it pop over the central frame. You can test to see whether the fabric is tight enough by tapping the top; if the fabric moves from the grasp of the hoops it is too loose and you will need to tighten the outer hoop and try again.

SLATE FRAME

The slate frame is comprised of four sections: two flat bars and two rolling bars. The two flat bars usually have a series of holes at either end, which are used to stretch the fabric as tight as possible. The two rolling bars have slots at either end that the flat bars slide into, and webbing attached down the centre of the bar (as shown right).

OTHER EQUIPMENT

Four nails or pegs

Bracing needle

String

Pins

Needle

Buttonhole or other strong thread

Webbing/herringbone tape

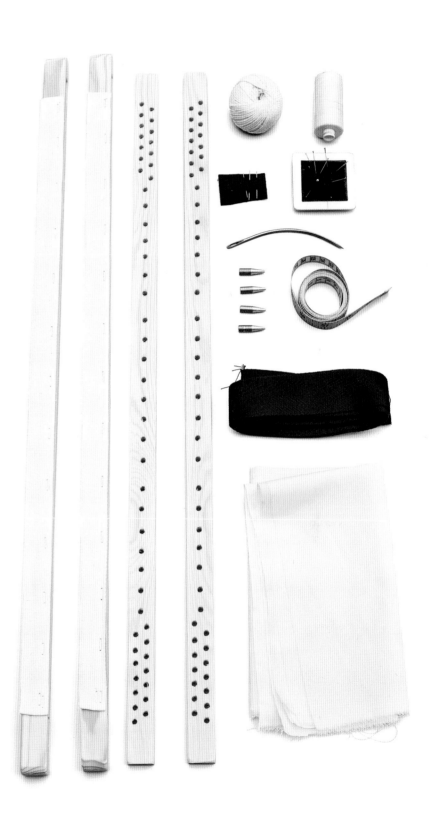

1 Take one of the rolling bars and find the central point of the webbing. Mark the central point with a pin or pencil mark.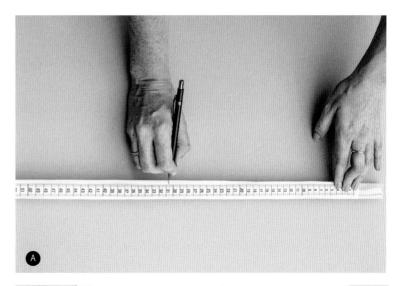

2 Take your fabric and make sure it is cut on each side as straight as possible down the grain, this will ensure that it will be completely flat once framed. If your fabric is not cut straight, your design will be distorted on the fabric and the embroidery tension will change once removed from the frame.

3 Find the central point of the top edge of the fabric. You can do this by folding the whole piece of fabric in half.

4 Place the central point of the fabric on the central point of the webbing.

5 Fold the fabric round the webbing so it sandwiches the webbing in-between.

6 Pin the fabric and the webbing together so they cannot come apart starting at the centre. Continue to pin all the way down one side then come back to the centre and repeat, going the other way. The pins should be about 3–4cm (1¼–1½in) apart.

7 Once the fabric has been pinned, take your needle and thread. Use a single thread and knot one end. Starting from the centre, start to stitch around the edge (oversewing) of the webbing and folded fabric (oversewing). As you move along you can remove the pins. Once you have reached the end of that side, start again from the centre and work out towards the other side.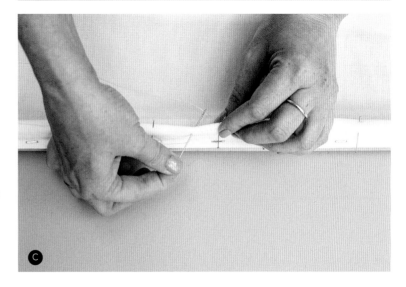

8 Once you have completed the whole length of the bar, you can use the same method to attach the fabric to the second rolling bar. Use the opposite (bottom) end of the fabric to attach the bar.

9 Insert the flat bars to the sides of the rolling bars, creating a square frame. Insert the pegs into the holes on each end of the rolling frames so the fabric is stretched as far as possible. 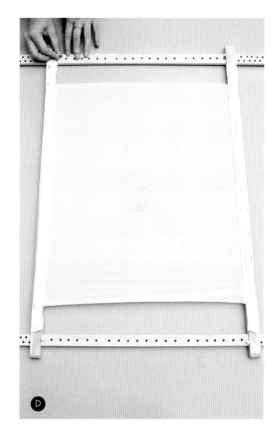 You many need to move the pegs out further as you go around and the fabric stretches.

10 Once the fabric is as tight as possible between the rolling bars you will need to stretch the fabric out to the flat bars. Measure the distance between the two rolling bars and cut some webbing or herringbone tape to that length.

11 Pin the tape half over the edge of the fabric and half off the side. Take a needle and single thread (the same as used before) knotted at one end, and make straight stitches approximately 1cm (½in) apart horizontally across the tape, sewing the fabric and the tape together (oversewing). As you move along you can remove the pins. Repeat this on both sides of the fabric.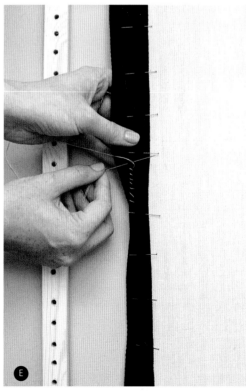

12 Take the bracing needle and thread it with the string (this can be normal parcel string). You will need approximately 10m (33ft) of string, but this can vary depending on the size of your frame.

13 Knot one end of the string, and starting from one side of the webbing, take the needle down through the overhanging tape. Now bring the string down under the flat bar at the side, over and then take the needle down through the webbing. As you are doing this pull the string tight so that the fabric is pulled flat. Repeat this all the way down the side of the fabric. **F**

14 Repeat to attach the fabric on the other side of the frame. Once complete your fabric should be taut and flat. **G**

15 Finally, you will want to check that the rolling bars are as far apart as possible. Turn the frame on its side and push both rolling bars apart; you may want to stand on the bottom bar with one foot to get the maximum stretch. If you are able do this you will need to move the pegs to a wider setting.

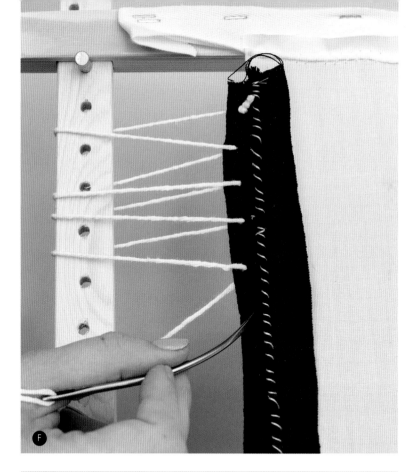

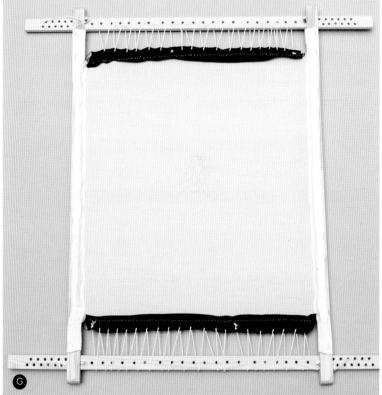

FRAMING UP A GARMENT

If you would like to embroider straight onto a garment you will need to frame support fabric on either a hoop frame of a slate frame (depending on the size of the embroidery). The support fabric will create the tension you need to embroider while allowing you to embroider on smaller areas that cannot be attached into a frame. If you are going to use goldwork, the support fabric could be calico or canvas (you should always keep the support fabric attached to the back of goldwork for extra strength); you would also use these fabrics if your garment is made from heavy fabric, such as denim. You can use lighter fabrics like tulle if the garment and embroidery will be light; the tulle or netting can then be cut away once your embroidery is finished.

1 Set up your chosen embroidery frame with the base fabric by following the steps described on pages 44–48.

2 Once you have your frame complete, you can take your garment and place it over the support fabric. Smooth out the area you would like to embroider so it is lying completely flat against the support fabric.

3 Pin the garment to the support fabric around where you are going to place your design. Try to stretch out the garment against the support fabric so it is taut like the frame.

4 Once you have pinned the fabric you will need a needle and strong thread. Knot one end of the thread and tack around your design where you have pinned. Once you have tacked all the way round you can then remove the pins. You will sew through both the fabric and the support fabric to give the embroidery extra support. Once the embroidery is complete you can cut the support fabric away.

TIP

If you are framing a transparent fabric, use a thin woven fabric as your support. Once the embroidery is complete you can pull the warp and the weft out from inside the embroidery.

BASIC EMBROIDERY STITCHES

WHICH STITCH?

Before embarking on your journey into learning the challenging aspects of embroidery, it is always good to learn a few of the basic stitches. These will help you to understand more complex and difficult stitches.

A lot of the embroidery used in fashion can quite often be very basic. You can achieve some beautiful effects with these stitches if you have the imagination to use them in the right context.

On the following pages you will find instructions on how to work the most common and versatile embroidery stitches, including favourites such as cross stitch (page 58), satin stitch (page 61) and French knots (page 63). Add to these a few straight stitches, as used on the flowers on the jeans shown opposite, and you can tackle almost anything.

If you'd like to take your embroidery up a notch, you will want to try long and short stitch (see page 74), which is also known as silk shading. Areas of long and short stitch are often outlined first in split stitch to give a very neat finish. This stitch is explained on page 57.

▶ Jonathan Simkhai (Spring/Summer, 2017) uses basic stitches such as running stitch and satin stitches with metallic thread to create a metallic feel to his garments.

MATERIALS AND EQUIPMENT

You can be really creative with the materials you use for these basic stitches, but always remember to think about the overall effect you want when making your choices. I would recommend learning these stitches on a small hoop frame. You can then move onto a larger frame if you are tackling a larger piece.

FABRIC

Choosing the right fabric for your embroidery is easy. You can pretty much use any fabric you like! The only thing to bear in mind is how heavy your embroidery will be; if you are going to do lots of heavy, dense stitching, it is probably best not to choose something light that will tear easily. I use a lot of denim, which is a great fabric to work with; it is strong and will not warp with the density of stitches.

THREADS

You can use a whole variety of threads for these stitches, which will create different effects. It is probably best to start with Anchor Stranded Cotton. This will allow you to try different thicknesses of thread depending on how many strands you use.

NEEDLES

Choosing your needle will depend on the thread and fabric you are using. If you are using a very thin thread it is best to choose a small needle, like a 10 or 12. If you want to embroider into leather you will need to choose a leather needle, and if you want to use thick threads a size 18 needle is best.

STARTING TO STITCH

Once you have compiled all your materials and set up your frame it is about time for you to embark on learning to embroider. It is always good to be patient as learning to embroider can sometimes be time consuming and frustrating. Remember always to take a step back and look at the overall effect of the embroidery and don't spend too much time with your face too close.

STARTING YOUR THREAD

I have heard a hundred versions of the right anchoring stitch to use, so I don't think there are any set rules regarding what you can and can't do. It is important to bear in mind that you want to keep the back of your fabric as neat and as bulk-free as possible; if you are using thick threads it is not advisable to have lots of knots at the back of the embroidery. The method I find the most effective and which does not make the back of the fabric untidy is the waste-knot method.

1 Thread your needle with a single thread, no longer than the distance from your hand to your elbow. Knot one end of the thread.

2 Choose an area inside where you will be embroidering and close to your starting point. Put your needle through the fabric so that the knot is on the top of the fabric; your anchoring stitches will be covered with embroidery once you start stitching.

3 Just next to your knot make three small straight stitches in the same place.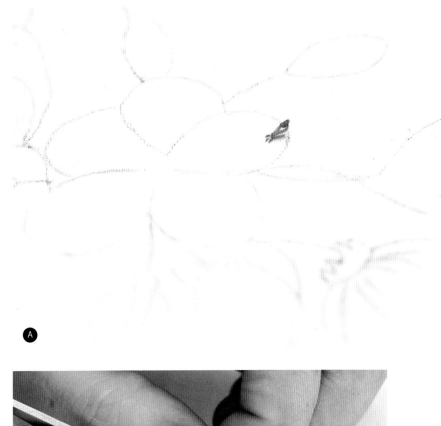

4 Once the thread feels as if it is secure, cut the knot off the top of the fabric, and you are ready to start stitching.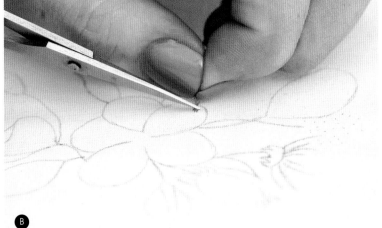

RUNNING STITCH

Running stitch is the most basic of embroidery stitches. It creates a single line of stitching that can be used to create decorative patterns. Each stitch is a simple straight stitch.

1 Bring your needle up at your starting point, then take your needle down in front of your starting point, at the length you would like to make your stitch.

2 Take the next stitch up through the fabric, just next to where you came down, and then move along so that the new stitch is the same length as the first.

3 Repeat steps 1 and 2, making sure your stitches are even. **Ⓐ**

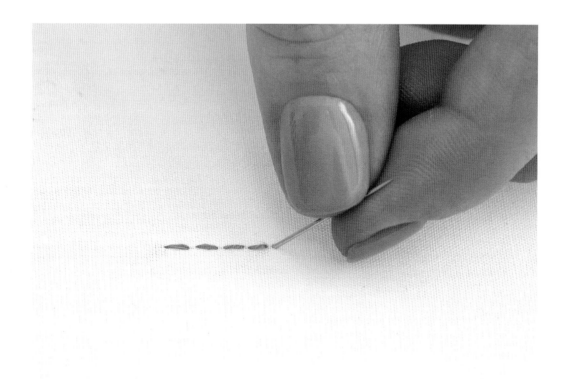

Ⓐ

SPLIT STITCH

Split stitch is usually worked around the outside edge of individual shapes to give definition and a smooth edge to work along. However, I love using this stitch with thick thread to create a decorative pattern along a cuff or hem.

1 To work the split stitch, bring your needle up at your starting point. Then take a stitch: the size of the stitch is up to you but I usually keep each stitch about 1cm (½in) long.

2 Underneath, move your needle back halfway along your first stitch. Bring your needle up through the middle of the stitch, splitting the thread in half.

3 Take your next stitch past the end of the first stitch and another half-length; go back down through the fabric and repeat step 2. **A**

4 Continue working in this way, keeping your stitches small and even. **B** When working around corners you may need to adjust your stitch length slightly so you start and finish exactly at the corner point.

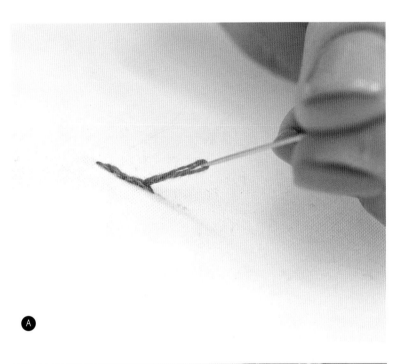

A

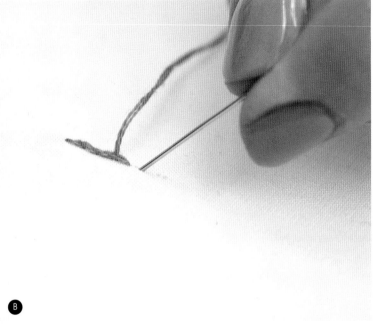

B

CROSS STITCH

Cross stitch is probably the most widely used embroidery stitch in the world. It can be used as a filling stitch to create block colour, or you can create detailed patterns in the embroidery. Cross stitch is embroidered onto an evenweave fabric. An evenweave fabric has the same amount warp and weft threads in 1 sq. cm. It is designed for counted stitches like cross stitch, so you can ensure that your stitches are even. Cottons and linens are the best evenweave fabrics to use for cross stitch.

◀ A great example of cross stitch used on the catwalk from Balmain (Autumn/Winter, 2012). Here cross stitch was used to created detailed floral images amongst heavy beading and appliqué.

1 Bring your needle up at the bottom-left corner of where you would like to make your cross stitch.

2 Count up and across an even number of fabric strands as if you were creating a square, and then take your needle down at the top-right diagonal corner.

3 From underneath the fabric, bring your needle up at the bottom right of the square. Ⓐ

4 Go diagonally up from this point to the top left-hand corner to create a cross.

5 From underneath, bring your needle up at the bottom right of the first cross, and repeat steps 1–4 to create your next stitch. Ⓑ

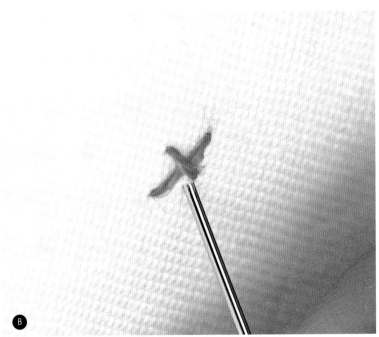

STEM STITCH

Stem stitch is a great stitch to create a rope or twisted-thread look. It is similar to split stitch but you will not be 'splitting' the thread.

1 To work the stitch, bring your needle up at your starting point. Take a small stitch down (approx. 1cm (½in), or however long you want you stitches. Do not pull the thread all the way through but leave a loop and hold it to one side.

2 Underneath, move your needle back halfway along your first stitch. Bring your needle up through the fabric, with the first loop of thread to one side. Then pull from the back of the fabric so the loop goes flat against the fabric and you can now draw your needle through. **Ⓐ**

3 Pull the thread all the way through the fabric then take your next stitch past the end of the first stitch and another half-length;, go back down through the fabric and repeat step 2. **Ⓑ** This time, your needle will come up at the end of the first stitch, and halfway along the second stitch.

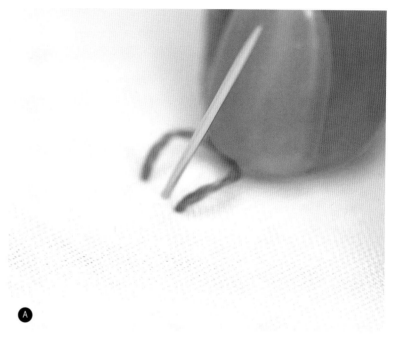

Ⓐ

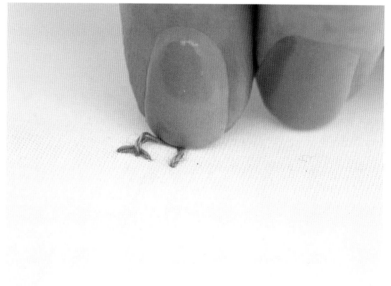

Ⓑ

60

SATIN STITCH

Satin stitch is a filling stitch that is used to cover an area of fabric. It can be used alongside a number of other embroidery techniques, such as goldwork and tambour beading.

1 To work the satin stitch, start in the centre of the area you would like to cover. Bring your needle up on one side of the area just on the outside of the design line.

2 Bring your needle over to the other side of the area and take your needle down.

3 Underneath, bring your needle back to the side you first started on, and come up right next to your first stitch; once again go over to the other side of the area and go down next to your other stitch. **(A)**

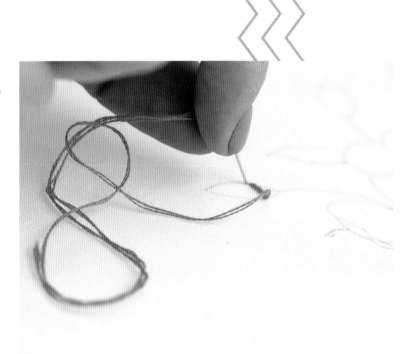

(A)

4 Make sure you keep your stitches as close as possible to one another; if they are not you will be able to see the fabric underneath. If you are going around corners you will want to space out your stitches slightly on the outer edge (not too much as the fabric below will be visible) and keep the stitches on the inner side really tight; this will allow you to embroider around the curve without overlapping stitches.

TIP

Draw directional lines on the fabric to help you make the stitches in the correct direction.

FRENCH KNOTS

French knots are great for creating texture on a garment, and are used in fashion embroidery more than they are given credit for. The knot is only comprised of one stitch so you can embroider lots of knots together to fill an area. You can also partially fill an area with French knots of one colour and then graduate another colour into them.

1   Bring the needle up at a point where you would like the knot to be. Holding the thread taut, wind the thread twice around the needle keeping it tight. **A**

2   Still holding the thread, take the needle down very close to point you came up at and pull the needle through to the back of the work; the twists will lie neatly on the fabric surface. The trick to French knots is tension – make sure you don't lose tension on the thread otherwise the knot will not be tight on the surface of the fabric. **B C**

LEAF STITCH

Leaf stitch is one of my favourite basic stitches. It works really well in floral patterns, hence the name leaf stitch. I often combine it with silk shading, with the silk-shaded flowers and the leaf stitch creating two different textures. The leaf stitch is known as a filling stitch, similar to satin stitch.

1 First you will need to mark out on the fabric the shape of your leaf. I also find it helpful to draw two lines down the leaf to represent each side of the central vein. These lines will also act as a guide as to where to place your stitches.

2 Bring the needle up at the base of the leaf on one side of the central vein. Take the needle across to the opposite side of the leaf and take the needle down on the outer edge. **A**

3 Bring the needle back up on the closest central line, take your needle across to the opposite side of the leaf and take it down on the outside line. **B**

4 Your third stitch needs to be made on the closest central line, near the first stitch, but positioned so that it will cross over the second stitch. Your third stitch should be parallel to your first stitch. **C**

5 Repeat this all the way up the leaf shape, keeping the spacing between each stitch the same size. As a final touch, you can outline the leaf with stem stitch.

A

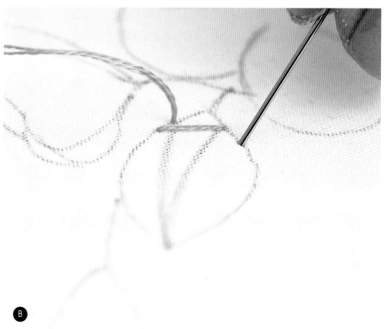

B

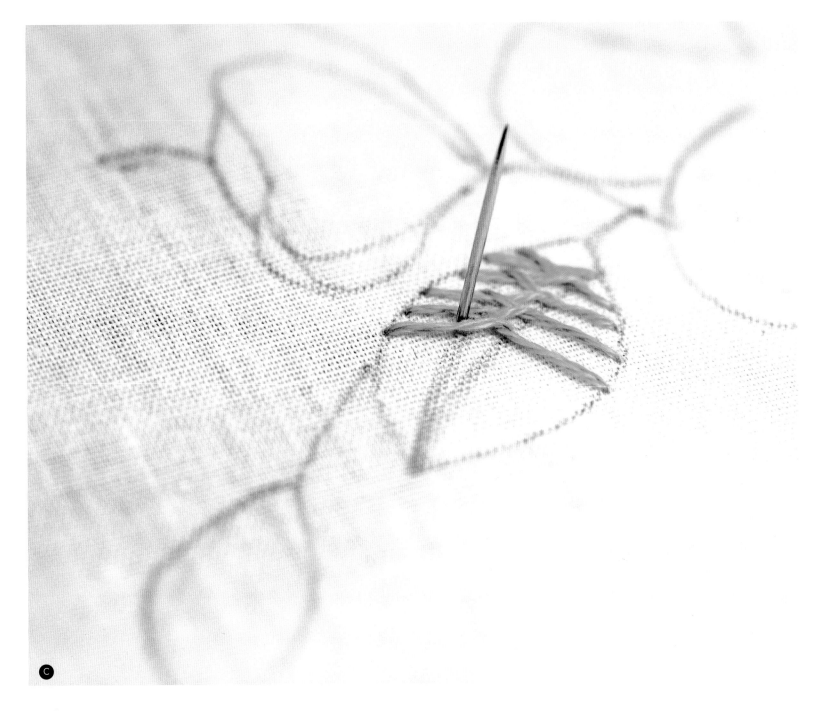

SILK SHADING

PAINTING WITH THREADS

Silk shading is known as painting with threads. It is very common in fashion embroidery and is used in all walks of fashion from haute couture to high street. At its highest level the technique can produce very lifelike effects.

Traditionally very fine threads are used to create the most lifelike representation; however, if you want to break with tradition thicker threads can be used to create a cruder effect. The technique of silk shading is comprised of long and short stitches, and is thought to be derived from satin stitch. The long and short stitches can be blended and shaded in different colours, hence the name silk shading.

◀ Silk-shaded flowers with beading detail by Ralph & Russo (Autumn/Winter, 2016)

▶ Silk-shaded embroidered flowers by Hand & Lock (Autumn/Winter, 2016).

▲ Hand-embroidered silk-shaded flowers and
petals by Oscar De La Renta (Spring/Summer, 2012).
These outfits represent many hours of silk-shading
embroidery but the effect is worth it.

▲ Andrew Gn (Spring/Summer, 2017).
Hand-embroidered, silk-shaded floral patterns on
silk chiffon (left) and on silk and cotton mix (right).

◀ Personalised jacket by Gucci (Autumn/Winter, 2015). Silk shading can be done on most fabrics except those with a lot of stretch.

MATERIALS

FABRIC

Silk shading can be worked on most fabrics, although I would recommend a satin or cotton to start with. I would advise avoiding stretchy fabric or those with a pile.

THREADS

I would always recommend starting with Anchor Stranded Cotton; this will allow you to play with the thickness of thread depending on how many strands you use.

NEEDLES

For very fine silk shading you will need to use a size 12 needle; thicker thread will require a larger needle.

OTHER EQUIPMENT

Scissors

Pencil

ORDER OF WORKING

With silk shading it is important to set out your order of work before starting. If you have a design with overlapping areas, the underneath layers of the design are worked first. You will then build up layers of work, completing the area that sits on top last.

STARTING TO STITCH

Thread your needle with a single thread, knotted at one end. Make sure your thread is never longer than from your hand to your elbow. There are many reasons for this: firstly, if your thread is too long, pulling it backwards and forwards through the fabric will put strain on the thread and eventually snap it; it also ensures that your thread will not get knotted while stitching and it will allow you to pull the thread through the fabric at the length of your arm and no longer.

SPLIT STITCH

Before going straight into using the long and short stitches you should first edge the areas that you are covering with split stitch. The split stitch will help create a clean and defined edge to the silk-shaded area.

LONG AND SHORT STITCHES

Before you start stitching, you may find it helpful to draw some
directional lines on your fabric with a pencil. If you do not want to
draw on the fabric you can do this on your line drawing design;
make sure you keep referring back to the design for guidance on
stitch direction. It is very easy to get the end of an area and realize
your stitches are not facing the correct way.

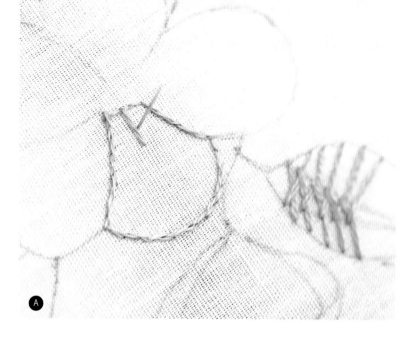

1   First work around the edge of the area you would like to fill with
split stitch. For a petal, your long and short stitches should be worked
from the base up. Your first stitch starts within the petal and goes down
to the lower edge. Bring your needle up at point A and down over the
split-stitch edge at point B. Keep the needle tucked in close to the
split stitch. **Ⅰ**

2   Bring your needle up at C and down at D. **Ⓐ** You will want to
make your stitch smaller than the first stitch; this will be your short
stitch. Then bring your needle up at E and down at F, making your
stitch longer. **Ⅱ** If you are working along a curve or angle, to help
achieve the angle, bring your needle out slightly further away and
take it down closer to the previous stitch at the bottom.

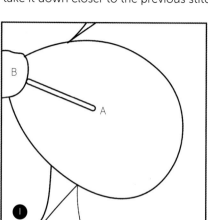
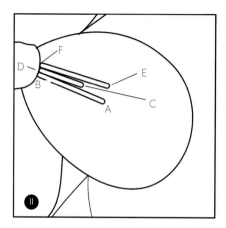
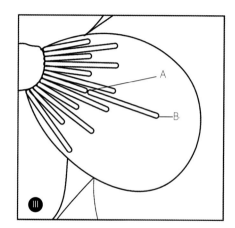

3 Continue working your stitches along the edge, making sure the split stitch is covered and the stitches are varied in length. Again, if you are working on an angle, your stitches should follow the direction of growth. Sometimes you may need to add a really small stitch just to help turn the angle if it is particularly sharp.

4 When the first row is completed the second row can be worked. From now on you work in the opposite direction. Bring your needle up at A, splitting the stitch from the previous row. Then take the thread down at B into the fabric. **Ⅲ**

5 Work the second stitch next to the previous one, again bringing your needle up in the previous row of stitches, splitting a stitch and coming down in the fabric. **Ⓑ**

6 Continue to work the second row, varying the length of your stitches on both ends. This will make sure they are blended into the first layer and will allow the next layer to blend with them.

7 Continue to work as many rows as required until the area is filled in. The more you vary the length of your stitches, the more depth you will create in your embroidery.

TIPS FOR SHADING AND BLENDING THE THREADS

When you want to change into a different colour, start a new needle with the new colour while keeping the previous one still attached to the fabric, then alternate between the previous colour and new colour for a couple of stitches so there is not an obvious change between the two.

This method can also be used when blending between the rows. Bring a stitch into the previous row in a different colour, so you aren't left with any obvious rows.

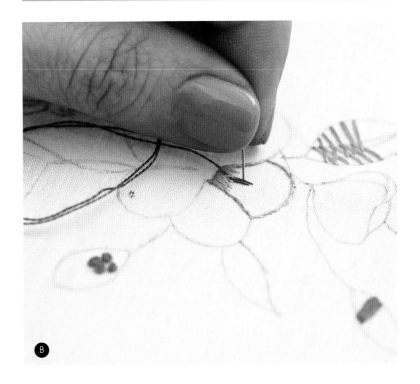

Ⓑ

GOLDWORK

PRECIOUS METALS

Goldwork is an embroidery technique that uses metal threads and bullions. Although its exact origins are not known, it is thought to have developed in Asia nearly 2,000 years ago, It became hugely popular in the Middle Ages when a style called *Opus Anglicanum* was developed by the English (see A brief history of fashion embroidery, page 14). After the Black Death killed about half the UK population during the 14th century, there was a decline in goldwork embroidery, but the 16th century saw a revival of the technique. Heavily embroidered garments became the usual attire for the rich; the typical gold-coloured embroidery was lavishly used, and thought to signify wealth and status. Since then goldwork has been used in many other settings, most recognizably in military and ceremonial uniforms.

The use of goldwork in high fashion is becoming a popular sight; companies such as Burberry and Dolce & Gabbana have used the technique to create military-inspired pieces.

▲ Goldwork crest for Burberry (Autumn/Winter, 2007), embroidered by Hand & Lock in varying colours of gold bullion and pearl purl. This intricate piece shows what can be achieved with cutwork.

▶ Ralph & Russo (Spring/Summer, 2016) have used goldwork materials with silk shading on the flowers to create wonderful textural contrast.

MATERIALS AND EQUIPMENT

There are lots of different materials to use in goldwork. Try not to get over excited and incorporate too many materials all in one design – it is better to pick one material that is used throughout your designs and highlight it with your smaller details.

FABRIC

Goldwork is a very labour-intensive technique, so choosing the right fabric is important. Preferred fabrics include satin, velvet, felt and canvas. Goldwork can be worked on light fabrics, but you will need to make sure that the embroidery will not rip the fabric if it is too heavy.

FRAMING

Because of the nature of goldwork and the heavy materials involved you will need to use a support fabric to give extra strength to the embroidery. You should always use a slate frame for goldwork, where you will initially frame up the support fabric, then attach the main fabric on top. The support fabric, usually a linen or canvas, will stabilize the embroidery while it is on the frame and ensure that it keeps its shape when released from the frame. To attach the main fabric to the support fabric I often use a fabric glue; this will allow you to make the main fabric really flat against the support fabric. Alternatively, you can stitch the main fabric to the support fabric (see page 49).

▶ Ralph & Russo (Spring/Summer, 2012) combine silk shading, beads and goldwork. Passing has been used for the finer detail around the edge of the leaves and flowers, while smooth bullion has been used to create the rippled detail in the centre. Blue beads have also been used to highlight the centre of the leaves.

METAL THREADS AND BULLION

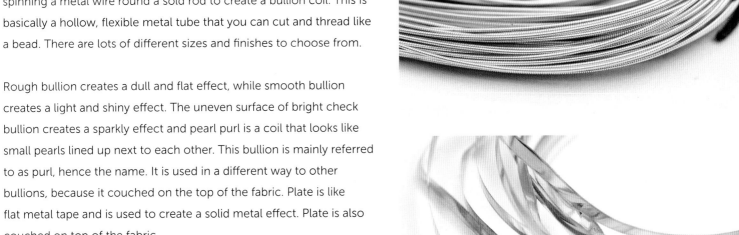

Although the name goldwork implies that the embroidery will be all gold, this is not actually the case. There are many different types and colours of bullion and metal threads that you can use to create an array of beautiful designs. To start with I have divided them into two basic categories: bullion and thread.

BULLION

There are a variety of names for this that you might come across when looking to purchase bullion. I have always used the term bullion, however you may come across names like cutwork threads and purl.

Bullion is one of the main materials used in goldwork. It is made by spinning a metal wire round a sold rod to create a bullion coil. This is basically a hollow, flexible metal tube that you can cut and thread like a bead. There are lots of different sizes and finishes to choose from.

Rough bullion creates a dull and flat effect, while smooth bullion creates a light and shiny effect. The uneven surface of bright check bullion creates a sparkly effect and pearl purl is a coil that looks like small pearls lined up next to each other. This bullion is mainly referred to as purl, hence the name. It is used in a different way to other bullions, because it couched on the top of the fabric. Plate is like flat metal tape and is used to create a solid metal effect. Plate is also couched on top of the fabric.

◀ Rough bullion (left) and smooth bullion (right).

▶ Bright check bullion (top), pearl purl (centre) and plate (bottom).

METAL THREADS

There are many different metal threads used in goldwork but the main one I use is called passing (see page 90). Passing has a thread centre that is wrapped with a metal foil to create the metal effect. It is used for couching, filling areas and creating detail. You can also buy other threads that need to be couched down, such as flatworm or check thread, very fine threads such as lurex thread that can be used to do the couching and finally embroidery threads like Anchor metallic embroidery thread.

◄ Passing is a metal thread used for couching, but I also find it useful for adding fine detail.

THREADS

There are no strict rules on what threads to use for goldwork, but you will need to choose a thread colour that matches your colour of bullion. For gold bullion you can use yellow thread, and for silver bullion you can use white thread. My preferred type of thread is Gütermann polyester thread for the bullion and Anchor metallic thread for the metal threads.

NEEDLES

Choosing the correct needle for your work is important. Your bullion will need a thin needle such as a size 12 so that it will slip through the centre of the bullion without getting stuck. The passing will require both a 10 or 12 needle and a larger chenille needle for plunging the thread. It may also be useful to have a curved needle to finish of threads at the back of your embroidery.

PADDING

Padding will allow you to create height and relief in your embroidery. There are two main types of padding: soft string padding and felt padding. Soft-string padding uses strands of soft string to create tapered shapes; the different strands will allow you to cut away sections in order to shape the area. String padding is mainly used underneath cutwork or plate. Felt padding is used to create an even height over a larger area – you can use multiple layers of padding to create different heights. Passing is the most common material to be used over felt padding as it can be couched over larger areas.

OTHER EQUIPMENT

Beeswax

Pounce powder

Pins

Rolled-up felt for pouncing

Scissors

ORDER OF WORK

Begin with your padding sections, then move on to the metal threads and cutwork.

STARTING TO STITCH

Always start with your plan. If you haven't already drawn up your design, refer back to pages 36–39. Next prepare your fabric, transfer your design (see page 40) and mount the fabric in a slate frame as described on pages 45–48. Now all you need is a place to stitch, a good light and very clean hands as the oils in your skin can tarnish the metal.

PADDING

Start off by applying the padding to the base fabric; if you do not want any padding under your embroidery you can move straight on to applying your bullion or metal threads.

FELT PADDING

1 Take your goldwork design that you have pricked, and pounce out the areas that need to be padded onto a piece of felt that matches the colour of the bullion or metal thread. Cut out the felt just inside the pounce line. If you would like multiple layers of padding you will need each layer of padding to be slightly smaller than the next – this will ensure that the padding will rise to the centre gradually.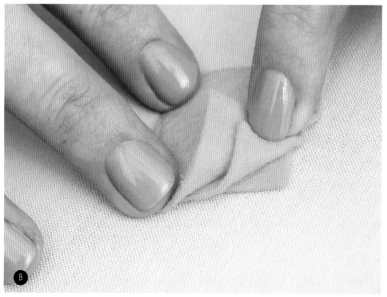

C

2 Starting with the smallest pieces of felt, place this in the centre of the area to be padded. Using a single thread, stitch all the way round the edge of the padding to hold it in place, making small stitches at right angles to the edge of the felt. Once your first layer is laid you can then build up your layers, gradually getting larger each time. Your final layer will need to be just smaller than the size of the embroidery area. **B** **C**

TIP

Keep your design in front of you while working; you can label the sections in number order so you keep track of where to go next.

SOFT-STRING PADDING

1 Measure the amount of soft string you will need by placing it over the area you want to fill; the soft string should cover the thickest area and also create height. Cut the soft string into lengths that are 3cm (1¼in) longer that the area you are going to fill.

2 Wax the soft string pieces; this will help to keep the separate strings together, making it easier to work with.

3 Lay the soft string over the area that needs to be padded. Using a double waxed thread, couch down padding from the centre first, bringing your needle up on one side of the string padding, over the padding at a 90-degree angle, and down on the other side. Remember to bring your needle up and down just inside the outer design line.

TIP

You can cut away more than one strand of string padding if the design tapers off quickly. However, do not cut off too much too quickly or you will be left with uneven padding.

A

B

4 Continue couching the soft string down, keeping the stitches tight and close together. When the shape starts to taper off, pull the string padding backwards and cut some of the soft string away from the centre underneath. **C**

5 Once cut, put the string padding back flat against the fabric, work another stitch and cut away more of the soft-string padding from underneath. Carry on in this way until you reach the point of the design. Here you should have cut off enough string padding from underneath that you should be left with only one strand.

6 Cut the last thread of padding to the correct length, then bring your needle up at the point of the shape and back down into the padding, securing the last strand. You can now go back to the centre of the design and continue to couch down the other side to the very point. **D E**

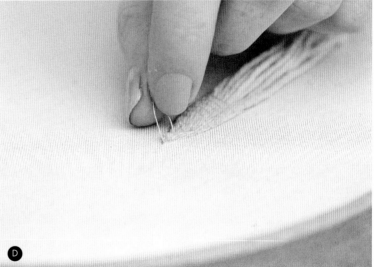

PASSING

Passing thread is used to fill an area by stitching it down (couching) using either the same coloured thread or a different coloured thread to create shading or a pattern in the couching stitches. It is usually applied over felt padding but can also be used over soft-string padding on occasion. If you prefer to have no padding, you can use it straight onto a flat surface. Passing can be couched down in pairs for quicker results, although for detail using a single strand is advised.

1   Start with a single thread and one or two strands of passing. Starting in the centre of the shape and working outwards, couch down the passing flat and try to keep it as straight as possible. Ⓐ

Ⓐ

2   Couch down the first row keeping the stitches about 3–4mm (1¼–1½in) apart and at right angles to the passing. When you reach the end of the design leave about 5–6cm (2–2¼in) of passing past the end of the design; this is so the passing can be plunged through the back of the fabric once the whole area is complete.

3   The next row can then be worked. Bring the needle up on the outside of the passing and then bring it down, angling the needle slightly under the previous row of passing. This will pull the two rows together. Make sure the stitches are sewn down in a brick pattern so that there is no obvious line of thread. Ⓑ

4   Continue stitching each row, couching over one or two passing threads to fill the padded area. Ⓒ

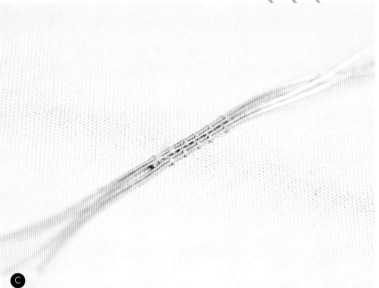

5 When the area is covered, the ends of the passing can be plunged to the back of the design. Using your chenille needle, thread the passing through this eye of the needle. Pull the needle and passing through to the back of the fabric, making sure you don't create a large hole in the front. Once you have pulled all the passing threads through to the back, turn to the back of the design and fold the passing back on itself. Then, using a double waxed thread, stitch over two of the gold threads at a time, catching the back of the fabric to hold them flat against the fabric. Stitch them down for about 1cm (½in), keeping the stitches close together. It may help to use a curved needle for this or alternatively, once your whole design is complete, it can be taken out of the frame and finished. Once you have done this you can cut away the excess passing. **D** **E** **F**

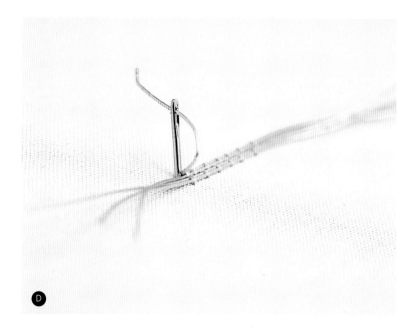

D

E

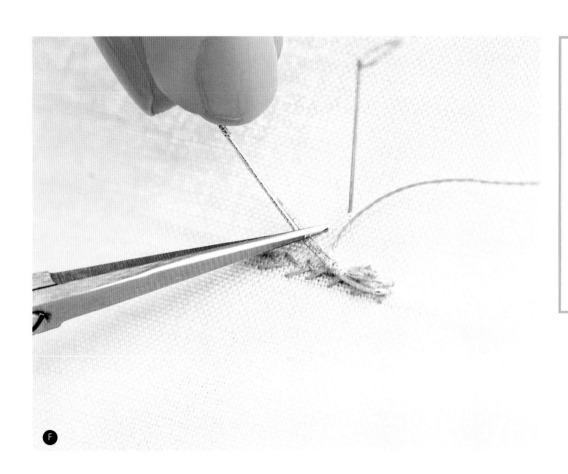

F

TIP

If you don't have a large chenille needle you can use a lasso to bring the passing to the back of the fabric. To do this, thread two ends of the same thread through a needle. Then take the needle down in the correct place and pass the passing through the loop that will be left. You can then bring the loop through to the back and the passing will follow.

CUTWORK

Cutwork is a technique using bullion that is cut into small sections and threaded, like a bead, onto your needle. It is usually done over a soft-string padded area, however you can also use cutwork over felt padding or flat. Cutwork is probably the most common goldwork technique used in fashion embroidery.

1   If you are using cutwork over soft-string padding you will want to start in the centre of the shape. For reference to cut the correct length bullion, lay the needle at a 45-degree angle across the padding to measure. Cut the correct length and stitch over the padding just outside the design lines on both sides. **A** **B**

2   Continue to work up the shape, always taking your needle up on one side and going down on the other. Make sure the bullion is cut to the correct size each time or you will end up with the bullion not sitting flat against the padding or, if it is too small, showing the padding beneath.

3   When you have completed one side, you can start again from the middle and work out. Continue to work in this way to the end of the design.

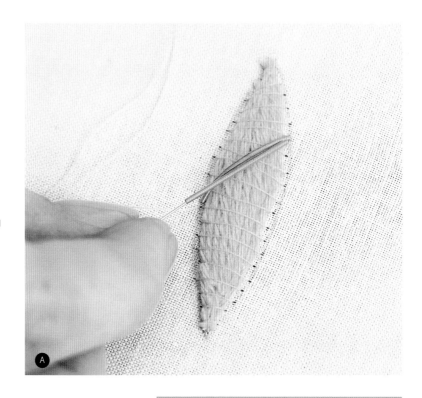

TIP

You can use a mellor to help lay the bullion down to stop it from cracking. If you don't have one, a large chenille needle or tapestry needle would also work.

PEARL PURL

Pearl purl is used mainly to edge an area of cutwork or chips (see page 98). It can also be used to mark an area or it can be used with different types of embroidery, such as silk shading and beading. The pearl purl is used in a similar way to passing as it is couched down on top of the fabric.

1   To start you will want to cut yourself a length of pearl purl that is about 6cm (2¼in) longer that the section you will be using it on. First, slightly stretch the pearl purl so that the small pearl-like sections are spread apart. Cut one end so that it has a clean edge and is ready to start with. **A**

2   Lay the pearl purl over the section you are going to start with. Using a single strand of waxed thread, stitch over (couch) the end of the pearl purl about 1cm (½in) in from the end. You will need to make sure that the thread drops in-between the sections, holding it tightly against the fabric. You should couch down the first section twice to keep it secure. **B**

3   Continue to couch down the pearl purl every three to four sections, with a double stitch at each end to keep it secure. When stitching, bring the needle up on the outside and down on the inside, angling the needle towards the inside to keep it tight against the area you are edging. **C**

4   When turning corners, use your needle or mellor to bend the pearl purl round to create the sharp turn. You will need to use a securing stitch to hold the corner in place and to keep the point as sharp as possible. When you have finished, carefully trim off the excess pearl purl.

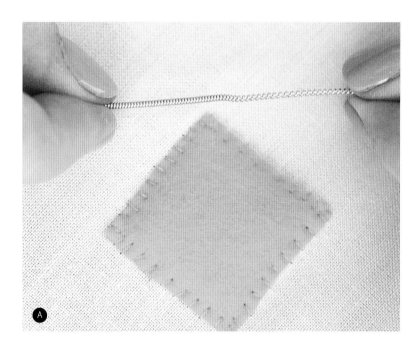

A

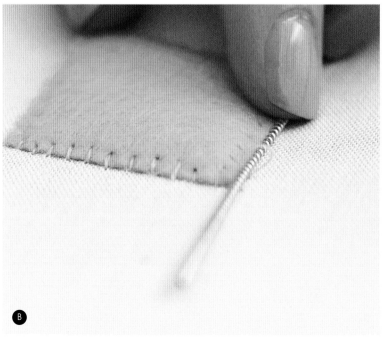

B

C

CHIPS

Chips are short pieces of bullion applied over a felt padded area; due to the nature of the small stitches you cannot use them over string padding. You would usually use bright check bullion to fill the area as it provides a shiny surface. It is great technique in goldwork as the small pieces create a reflective surface, and when the fabric moves it will glisten in the light.

1 Before applying the chips you will want to edge the area you are filling with pearl purl; this will give a clean edge to your chips.

2 Cut the bright check to lengths of about 2mm (1/16in). Using a double waxed thread, stitch each chip down like you would a small bead. Make sure that all the chips are close and lie at different angles so there is no padding showing through. The area needs to be encrusted to give it a rich and lustrous texture. **A**

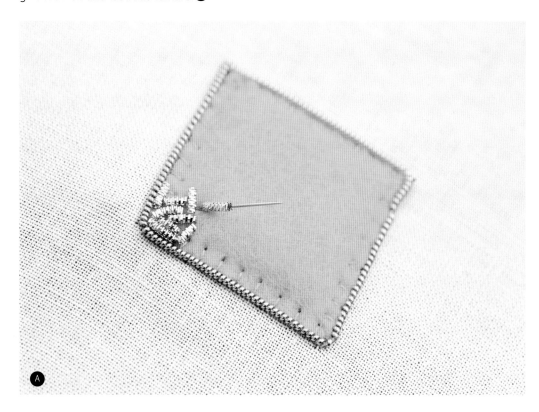

A

ESSING (S-ING)

This is a very similar stitch to stem stitch; it gives the same effect but is executed slightly differently. Essing is mainly used to edge or mark out areas or details. It can also be used in rows to create a pretty, feathered appearance.

1   Bring your needle up at your starting position. Cut small, equal lengths of bullion and thread one onto your needle.

2   Take your needle down through the fabric at the length of the cut bullion. From behind, move your needle in front, half the length from your last stitch and come back through the fabric.

3   Thread your needle with another small length of bullion – this should be the same length as before. Push the bullion all the way down so it is against the fabric.

4   Take your needle back to your previous stitch and go down underneath the last piece of bullion. You will want to go down in the middle of the bullion, angling your needle so you can get as far underneath as possible.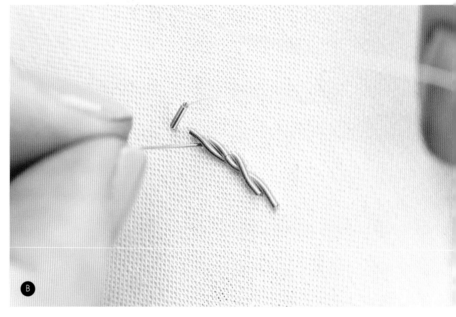

5   Continue to repeat steps 2–4.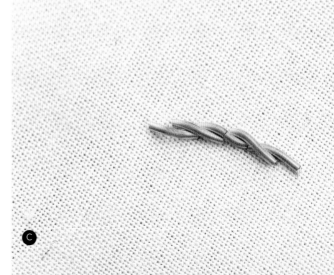

TIP

You can use different coloured bullion to create a multicoloured effect – alternating rough and bright check, for example.

PLATE

Plate is a flat metal strip that can be woven, interlaced, coiled, folded or pleated. It can be folded in tight folds with no gaps, or spaced out to create a zigzag effect.

1 Bring your needle up at the point you would like to start, laying your plate under your needle, with approximately 5mm (¼in) on the inside of the embroidery area. Take the needle down over the plate and through the fabric (couch).

2 Pull the thread tight so it keeps the plate in place. Work a small stab stitch for added security, if desired. **A**

3 Fold the plate over the stitch and over the embroidery area.

4 Bring your needle up on the topside of the plate and couch this in place. **B**

5 Fold the plate back over the embroidery area and take another stitch over the plate to hold it in place.

6 Continue to fold and couch the plate in place until you have covered the embroidery area.

▶ Hand & Lock have used silver plate along the rays of a star to create a solid metal effect. The plate has been edged in Purl Pearl to give a clean finish.

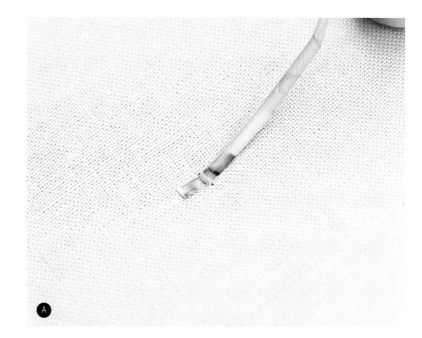

A

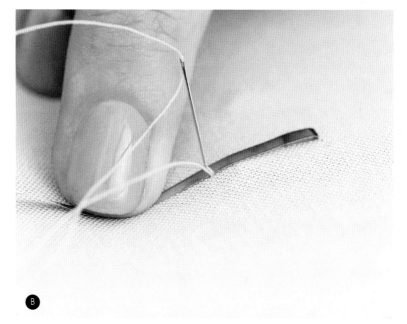

B

TAMBOUR BEADING

BEADS AND SEQUINS

Also known in France as *crochet de Lunéville*, and Zari or Aari work in India, tambour beading is a technique that uses a hooked needle to create chain stitches that incorporate the use of beads, sequins or pearls. The difference between the European technique and the Zari work is that tambour beading attaches beads from the spool thread on the reverse side of the fabric, leaving the chain stitch on the top; Zari work attaches the bead from the needle onto the front of the fabric.

The technique was invented in Lunéville, France, in the early 19th century. It was originally used to imitate lacework, but was later developed to be used on garments by adding pearls within the chain stitch.

The name tambour beading is derived from the French word 'tambour' meaning 'drum'. The stitch is worked into fabric that is stretched over a tight frame, creating a drum-like effect. Unlike other embroidery techniques there is only one stitch in tambour beading – the chain stitch. The advantage of using the tambour beading chain stitch over individually stitching down beads is speed. Although it can take time to learn and is difficult to master, once the technique is executed properly it will provide a fast and effective way of attaching beads.

Tambour beading is one of the most popular techniques used in fashion embroidery, and has become the embroidery language of haute-couture houses. It is used by designers all over the world to create intricate and versatile embroidery. It is my favourite embroidery technique and, although it will take a while to pick up, please be patient and keep trying – I promise it will eventually click!

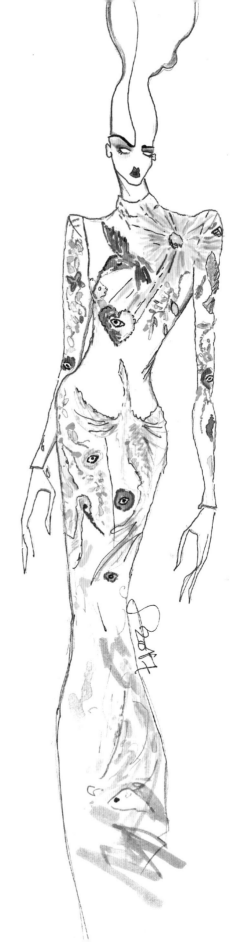

◀ ▲ Alexander McQueen made great use
of tambour beading in his 2016 collections.
Beads and sequins featured to stunning effect in
Spring/Summer (left) and were carried through to
the Autumn/Winter collection (above and right).

◄ ▲ Marchesa Autumn/Winter 2017 (left) and Spring/Summer 2017 (above). Both pieces use tambour beading for detailing with a combination of other appliquéd materials.

▲ Naeem Khan (Spring/Summer, 2016). Heavily tambour beaded in sequins. The sequins have been stitched flat next to each other rather than overlapped to cover the area without making the dress too heavy.

▲ Pamella Roland (Autumn/Winter, 2017). Tambour beaded with square bronze sequins and small seed beads. Larger backed crystals have been used as detail in between and sewn on by hand.

MATERIALS AND EQUIPMENT

Gathering your materials for tambour beading can sometimes be difficult as the correct materials are hard to come by. Invest in a good-quality hook and holder so learning to stitch will be easier. You will also want to find good-quality beads and sequins – you don't want to let your embroidery down by poor-quality materials.

FRAME

You will need to make sure you have a really tight frame for tambour beading. I usually use a slate frame to keep my fabric as tight as possible. You will need to frame your embroidery so the reverse side of the fabric is facing upwards; this is because you will work from underneath. With transparent fabric this should not matter, but bear this in mind when framing opaque fabric.

FABRIC

Tambour beading is a versatile technique and can be used on many different fabrics. To start with you will want to use transparent fabric, then once you feel comfortable with the technique you can move on to opaque fabric. It is best to start with silk organza – a strong sheer fabric – as this will allow you to make mistakes and rectify them easily without ruining the fabric.

BEADS AND SEQUINS

Tambour beading allows you to use a huge variety of beads and sequins, but you will always need to make sure that the ones you use have a hole all the way through. Beads with a clasp or no hole at all cannot be used for tambour beading. You will also want to try to buy your beads or sequins strung onto a thread.

THREADS

There are many different types of thread you can use for tambour beading. I always advise using a cotton or cotton-polyester mix glacé thread; this is a polished or lubricated thread that will allow you to move smoothly through the front and back of the fabric without splitting the thread.

TAMBOUR HOOK AND HOLDER

Your needle is comprised of two sections; the tambour holder and the tambour hook.

TAMBOUR HOLDER: This is usually a wooden vice that will hold your hook in place. They come in different sizes and shapes but you will want to find the one that feels most comfortable in your hand. 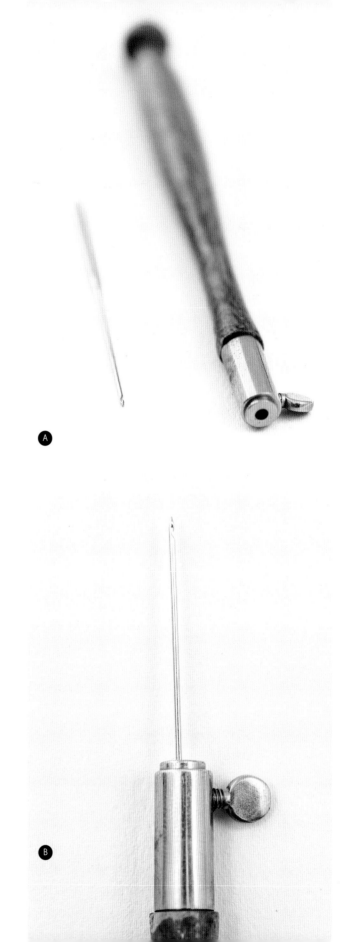Ⓐ

TAMBOUR HOOK: This is a needle with a small hook on the end. The needles come in various different sizes to suit different fabrics and stitch sizes. These range from 70 (smallest) to 120 (largest). Start with an 80, which will allow you to create a fine, clean chain stitch and will also allow you to attach beads. Ⓑ

On your holder, there will be a small screw towards the top. Unscrewing this will allow you to put the hook into the holder. Tighten the screw shut so the needle is firmly in the holder. You will need to make sure the front of the hook is in line with the screw; this is really important as once the hook goes through the fabric the screw will be your only point of reference for the way the hook is facing.

TIP

You may want to cut the needle down if you feel it is too long. It is advisable to have the hook about 2–3cm (¾–1¼in) out from the top of the holder to give you greater control over the hook.

Ⓐ

Ⓑ

PREPARATION

Preparation is key: take your time in framing up your fabric correctly and transferring your design onto the fabric so it will not be visible under clear beads or sequins. An invisible or wash-away pen is always useful for this.

TIP

Remember you are now working on the back of your fabric so you will need to transfer your design backwards to make sure it is the right way round on the front of the fabric.

TRANSFERRING YOUR DESIGN

As you are working from the back of your fabric you will want to make sure you transfer your design onto the reverse of your fabric as this will be the side you will see.

For beginners, you will be working on organza fabric, which is transparent. You can transfer your design just by placing the design underneath the organza and using a fine pencil to draw over it.

If you are working on opaque fabric you will need to prick and pounce your design on to the back of the fabric (see Transferring your design, page 40).

Before starting to stitch I would advise taking some time to get used to the hook. You may not be used to your needle having a hook on the end and it is good to familiarize yourself with the feeling of the hook coming through the fabric.

Take your hook in the hand that you write with; hold it vertically above the fabric and then lower the needle into the fabric. Pull the needle vertically back up though the fabric, trying not to catch the hook on the fibres. Do this a few times until you feel comfortable with how this feels.

The first thing to remember with tambour beading is that you do not cut your thread – it will stay attached to the reel, so make sure you find a good place to keep it (see tip, opposite).

CASTING ON

Casting on and off is probably the hardest part of tambour beading as the chain stitch is so small. If you are struggling to master this, put a pin in the fabric and wind the thread around the pin to secure it. You can go on and master the chain stitch and come back to this once you are ready.

1 Take the hook to the place where you would like to start. Push the hook down through the fabric. With your hand underneath, loop the thread onto the hook. **A**

2 Hold the loop with your hand and then pull the hook back through the fabric. You can then let go of the tail thread so it comes all the way through to the front of the fabric. **B**

3 Holding the tail thread in place on the front of the fabric, take the hook down on the line, slightly further away from where you started. Make sure the hook and small screw are facing the direction you want to travel in. Remember that your screw is the point of reference for the way the hook is facing. Push the hook through the fabric. **C**

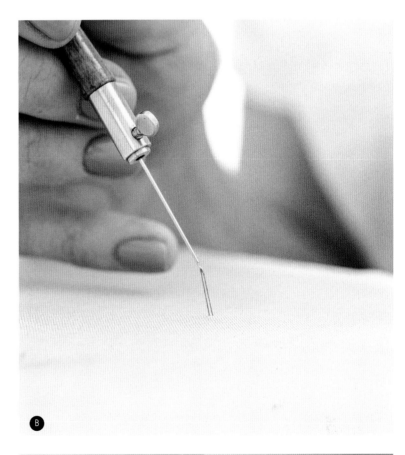

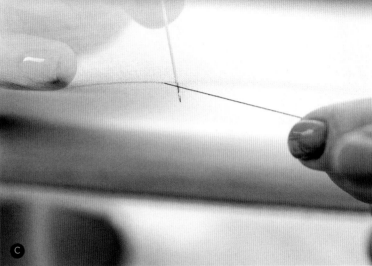

TIP

It is easiest to start with the direction of travel towards you.

4 On the underside of the fabric, wrap the thread clockwise 360 degrees around the hook so the thread is coming from the same direction in which you are travelling. You can now twist the hook clockwise 180 degrees so the screw and hook are facing away from the direction that you are travelling. Pull the tambour hook back through the fabric to create a small thread loop on the top of the fabric. **D** **E**

TIP

If you have trouble getting your hook out of the fabric, push it back slightly as you lift it so that the hook clears the hole more easily.

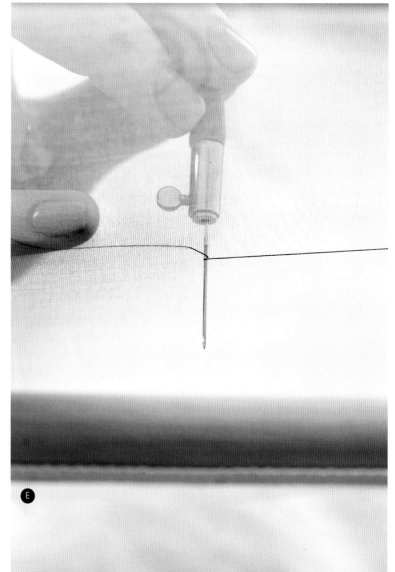

5 Bring the needle backwards, away from your original direction of travel, and take it down next to your tail thread. Try to keep the stitch as small as possible. **F**

6 Again, wrap the tail thread clockwise 360 degrees around the hook and pull the loop through to the front, remembering to turn the hook clockwise 180 degrees away from where you came through before.

7 Now turn the needle back to the original direction of travel and come back down just next to your first loop. **G**

8 Repeat step 4, then for the final step take the needle down next to the top stitch and repeat step 4–6. You are now cast on and ready to start the chain stitch.

Casting off will be exactly the same as casting on, but backwards. Essentially casting on is three small stitches backwards and forwards, so, to cast off at the end of the section you have finished, use the same 3–4 small stitches backward and forward. Then pull the last loop through and cut it, releasing the spool thread from underneath.

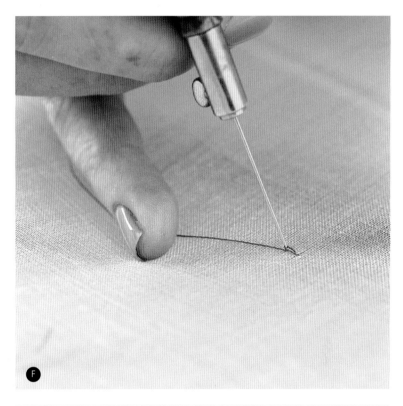
F

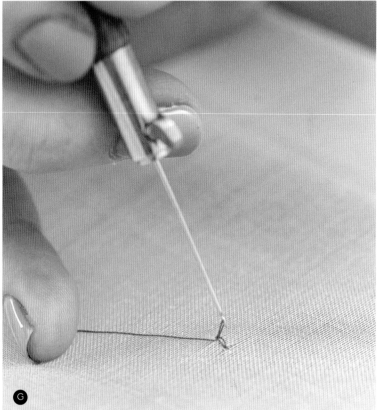
G

CHAIN STITCH

The chain stitch is fairly simple. If you have already managed to tackle casting on then you will have already done a few chain stitches.

The chain stitch can be used as a decorative stitch, not just a stitch to attach beads, so don't be afraid to use it when designing your pattern. As mentioned above, tambour beading is worked from the back of the fabric, but if you would like to use the chain stitch as a decorative stitch, you will need to work on the front of the fabric so the chain stitch sits on the top.

1 If you have already cast on you should have a loop on your hook ready to go, if not, you will need to drop your needle into the fabric at the position you would like to start. Loop the thread underneath onto the hook and pull through the fabric to create the loop on the top. (See step 1 of Casting on, page 113). **A**

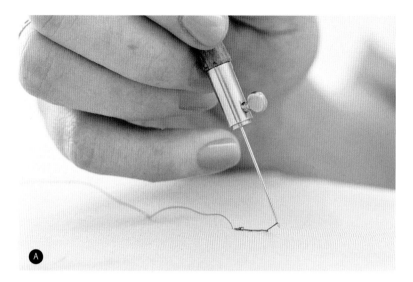

2 From your casting-on knot, or where you have just come up with your loop, put your needle down just in front of the knot/loop and through the fabric (this will make sure you hide the knot). Make sure when you go down your needle is facing the direction of travel (the direction you are going to carry on stitching). Remember it is easiest to start the with direction of travel towards you. **B**

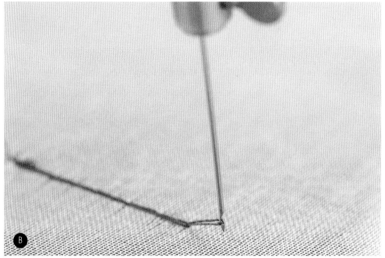

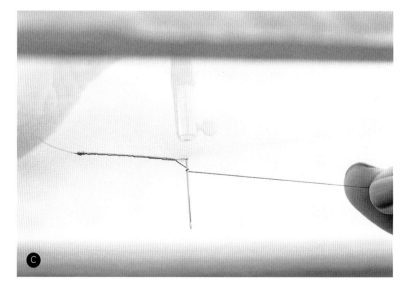

3 Take the thread from behind your needle and wrap it clockwise 360 degrees round your needle. **C** Now turn your needle 180 degrees clockwise to face the opposite direction. **D**

4 Bring your needle back through the fabric, creating a loop on the top of the fabric. **E**

5 Now turn your needle back to the direction of travel and repeat. **F** You should now begin to see the loops interlock with one another creating a chain stitch. Practice the chain stitch until you feel comfortable with all the steps. It is good to try out different sized stitches in different directions.

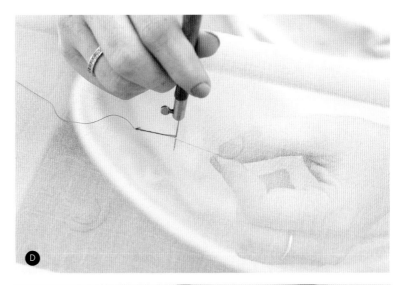

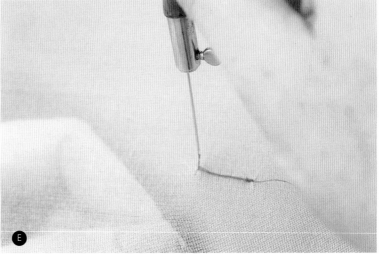

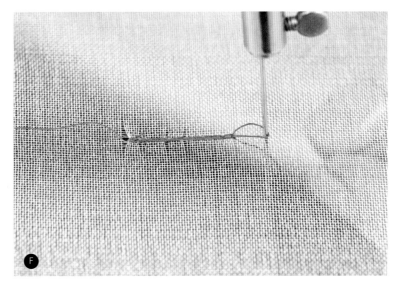

TIP

When your loop is at the top of the fabric, twist your needle back the opposite way to ensure that there is not twist in your loop.

TROUBLESHOOTING

There are a number of issues that you might face when trying to master the chain stitch so here are some of the most common.

I AM STRUGGLING TO COME BACK THROUGH THE FABRIC: This happens a lot when starting to learn tambour beading. It is important to keep your hook and holder at a 90-degree angle to the fabric to ensure that it will pass through smoothly. You will also want to put a bit of pressure on the back of the needle to allow the fabric to warp open and the needle to pass through. Remember the hook is at the end of the needle so make sure you apply the pressure until the needle is fully through the fabric. If you get stuck coming out of the fabric, push your needle back through and try to come back, do not try to rip the hook through as this will damage your fabric.

MY THREAD IS SPLITTING: When your needle is through the fabric and you wrap the thread 360 degrees around your needle, make sure that the thread loop around your needle drops into the hook before pulling the needle back through the fabric. Ⓐ If you pull the needle through the fabric before dropping the thread into the hook you will risk the hook splitting the thread. This happens when the hook pulls half of the thread to one side of the fabric and leaves the other half behind.

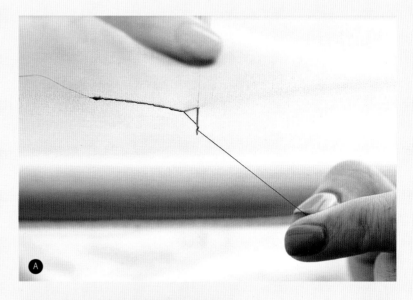

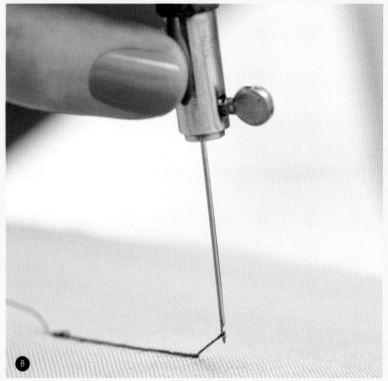

I KEEP DROPPING MY STITCH WHEN I COME THROUGH THE FABRIC OR WHEN I AM ABOUT TO GO BACK DOWN: When you come through to the top of the fabric the loop will only be attached to the hook on your needle so you will need to make sure the loop is all the way round the needle. **B**

I GOT THE HANG OF THE CHAIN STITCH AND NOW I AM STRUGGLING: Check your screw and hook are in line. When you are using the hook and holder a lot they can sometimes become misaligned, making it difficult to judge which way your hook is facing.

I AM CATCHING ON THE PREVIOUS LOOP WHEN COMING THROUGH TO THE FRONT: Once again, this could be an issue with the hook and the holder not being aligned, but it could also be that when you are coming back through the fabric your screw is not in line with the opposite direction of travel. You should always make sure that you hook goes down in the direction of travel and comes back through in the opposite direction (180 degrees). **C**

WHEN I AM COMING THROUGH THE FRONT OF THE FABRIC THE LOOP IS NOT COMING WITH ME: Make sure the tension of your thread underneath is tight enough to keep the loop wrapped round the needle when you come through the fabric. If it is too loose the loop with fall away when you pull through.

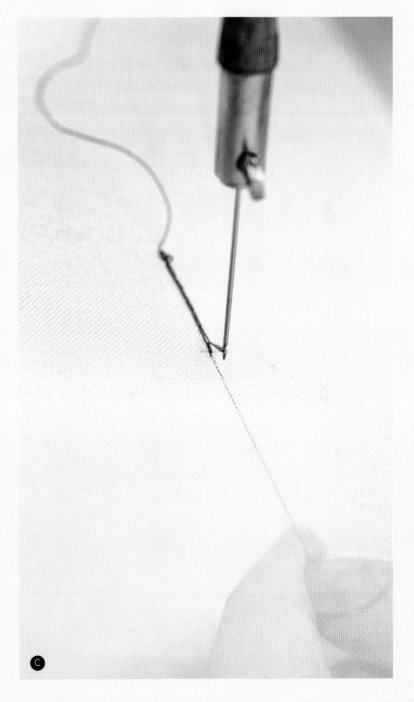

C

119

ATTACHING BEADS

Once you feel as if you have got the hang of the chain stitch you can move on to attaching your beads. I would always suggest starting with a bugle bead or large circular bead, as these will be the most straightforward. Once you feel comfortable you can move on to other smaller beads. You will need to start by stringing your beads onto your spool thread. You can do this with a bead stringer or you can buy beads that are already strung.

If you buy beads already strung you will need to move them over to your spool thread. You can either do this by tying the two threads together and passing them over the knot onto the spool thread (this will not work for small beads) or using the following method.

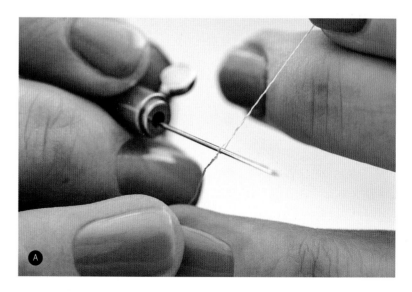

MOVING BEADS ONTO SPOOL THREAD

1   Take the thread that your beads are attached too, and, using your tambour hook, split the thread in half. Do not spilt the thread too close to the end as it will end up splitting the thread all the way down; you may need to remove some beads to give you space. **Ⓐ**

2   Loop the spool thread onto the end of your hook. **Ⓑ**

3   Pull the hook with the spool thread attached through the split thread. You can now pull the tail end of the spool thread all the way through the spilt thread. **Ⓒ Ⓓ**

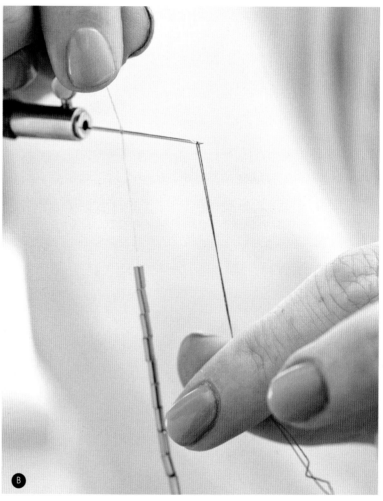

4 Drop both the spool thread and the split end of the thread with your beads on it, pick up the other end of the thread with beads and hold it high up. You can now push the beads from the split thread to the spool thread.

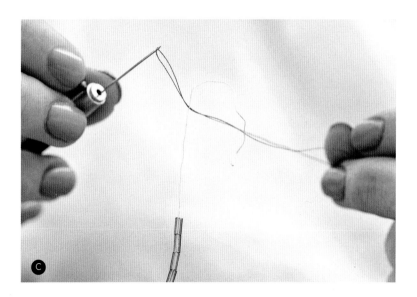

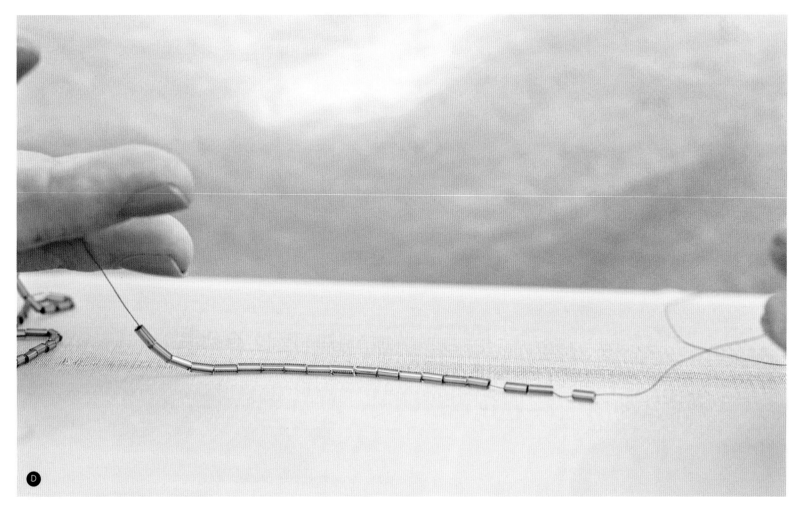

HOW TO ATTACH BEADS

Now your beads are attached to your spool thread you are ready to start attaching the beads to your fabric. You will use the same method for the chain stitch as before, but this time you will be adding a bead in the middle of the process.

1 Cast on as normal, then push up one of the beads from your spool thread underneath so it is touching the back of the fabric. **A** Remember the front of your fabric is underneath so the beads will be attached from below. Then take your hook down in front of the bead. You can use the size of the bead as reference for how big your stitch will need to be; however, you will need the stitch to be a tiny fraction bigger than the bead. If it is too long the bead will slide up and down the thread. If the stitch is too small the beads won't lie straight and will start to sit on top of one another.

2 Wrap the thread 360 degrees around the hook on the other side of the bead, keeping the thread tight, and the bead flat against the back of the fabric. **B** Before you bring the hook back through the fabric, turn the hook so that it faces the opposite way to the direction of travel, just as before.

3 Pull the hook upright through the fabric so the bead is now secured on the other side of the fabric. Be careful not to drop the loop here as the weight of the beads will pull the chain stitch out.

4 Again turn the hook back to the direction of travel, push a bead up to the back of the fabric and take the hook down just behind it. Continue as described in steps 2 and 3 to complete another stitch.

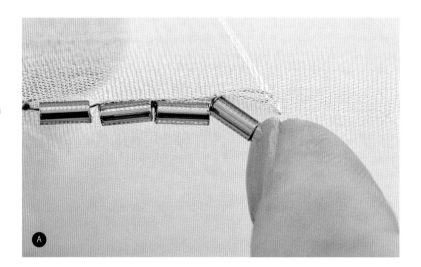

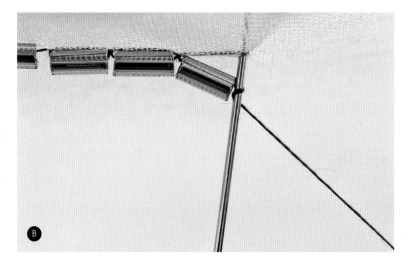

▶ Tambour-beaded piece, embroidered by Hand & Lock in seed beads, sequins and bugle beads. The chain stitch has also been used as a decorative stitch between the black seed beads.

ATTACHING SEQUINS

You will need to transfer your sequins over to your spool thread as you did for the beads. Many sequins will have a wrong and a right side; you will need to transfer your sequins over to your spool thread so they will be the correct way up. If you find the front of your sequin you will need to make sure they are transferred over with the front facing towards the spool.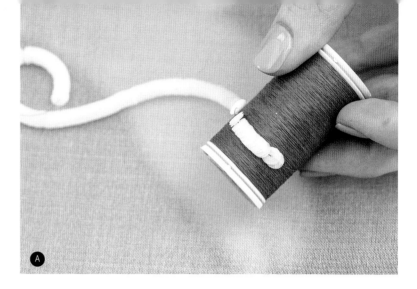

Sequins are attached in the same way as beads but instead of making the stitch slightly larger you need to make the stitch half the size of your sequin – this will ensure your sequins overlap one another. Take care not to attach more than one sequin. It can be very easy not to separate them properly. If you do not want to make your sequins overlap you can make the stitch the same size as your sequin and they will lie flat next to one another. **B** **C**

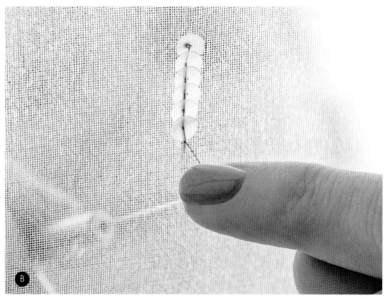

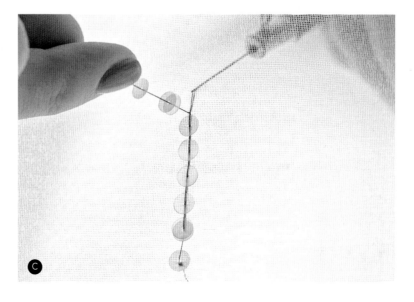

TURNING CORNERS

If you want to make a sharp turn on a corner you will need to make an anchor stitch to hold the corner sequins in place. Once you have made your stitch into the corner you will need to do a very small stitch to hold the previous stitch in place. This will anchor down the last stitch and allow you to move off in the other direction.

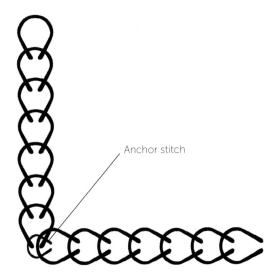

Anchor stitch

USING OTHER MATERIALS

UNUSUAL MATERIALS

You don't always have to use traditional techniques or materials in embroidery. These days a lot of embroidery uses unconventional materials to create new and exciting effects. If you have the experience in the traditional techniques, it will inform you how to incorporate new materials. I have worked on pieces at Hand & Lock where I have created lifelike replicas of objects in embroidery. I have used cut-up paintbrush bristles to create the look of hair, and 3D-printed interlocking beads that shape around the body. It is good to get creative with the techniques and materials you use and create your own style so that you can explore the endless possibilities embroidery offers.

3D EMBROIDERY

Embroidering flat on fabric may not give you the depth that you require. By building layers of fabric on top of a base fabric you can create another dimension for your garment, although this is not always thought of as embroidery but rather as fabric decoration. I like to think that you can combine elements of traditional embroidery techniques into the layers of fabric to create something new. 3D beading is something that is also a step away from the traditional techniques of embroidery but is used heavily in the world of fashion embroidery. Here I will show you two different styles of 3D flowers and some 3D beading. These techniques can be applied to any shape or style you like.

▶ Alexander McQueen (Spring/Summer, 2017). Small flowers have been created with sequins and 3D bugle beads. Larger flowers have been created by layering different types of fabric to create the layers of petals.

128

◀ ▲ Nguyen Cong Tri (Autumn/Winter, 2017) uses a mixture of hand and hand-guided machine embroidery to create detail in his foliage. He then uses bugle beads between the layers of fabric to create the 3D effect while also using pleats and gathering to create height in the embroidery.

3D FLOWERS

3D flowers are commonly used in fashion embroidery. There are lots of techniques to achieve a similar effect, but here I have chosen two styles that I use most commonly in my fashion embroidery.

STYLE 1

You will need two pieces of fabric for this style. The first piece of fabric will be your base fabric – if you would prefer to do the embroidery straight onto a garment this will be the fabric of the garment. I would suggest using a heavier fabric for your base that will support the embroidery; netting will not be suitable. The second piece of fabric will be for your flower. I would usually use a light organza or silk for this; anything too heavy will fall flat onto the base fabric.

You will also need an embroidery frame, a needle (size 10 or 12), Anchor Stranded Cotton, scissors, pounce powder, tracing paper and a pencil. Also useful (although not essential) are multi-purpose thread, bugle beads, seed beads and thin wire.

1   Put your base fabric to one side as you will not need this straight away. Taking the other piece of fabric, you will need to prick and pounce (see Pricking and pouncing, page 41) or draw the shape of the petals you would like to embroider. I would recommend drawing about 5–6 petals of different sizes so you can layer them on top of each other.

A

2   You will need to mount your petal fabric onto a frame. I would usually use a hoop frame for small petals. If you would like large petals that do not fit into the hoop frame you will need to frame up a slate frame. (See Setting up your frame, pages 44–48)

3   Inside the petal you will want to embroider the detail. You can do this in many different ways, however, I like to keep it simple and only embroider the central veins towards the bottom of the petals. I usually use long and short stitches of different colours to create a blended effect. A

4   Once you have enough embroidered petals for your flowers, cut the petals out so you can attach them to the base fabric. You will need to secure the edges so they don't fray. There are two options that produce different finishes as explained on pages 134–135.

5 Now your petals are ready to be stitched down to the base fabric. Frame up your base fabric in either a hoop frame or a slate frame (see Setting up your frame, page 44–48). Placing the larger petals on the base fabric first, lay the bottom of the petal where the centre of the flower will be.

6 Taking the same thread you have used for the detailing on the petal, secure the petal to the base fabric. Using long and short stitches work into the petal and the base fabric so your stitches blend into the petal. **B**

7 You can then place each petal over the top of the next to create the whole flower. **C**

8 Once you have a completed flower you can add detail into the centre of the flower; I usually use French knots and upright bugle beads (see 3D beading, page 139).

B

C

TIP

If you want to add more body to the flowers you can also add a small wire into the petal hems. This will allow you to shape each petal once stitched down.

HEMMING PETALS (OPTION 1)

This option gives the petals a clear, sharp edge. Do the stitching before you cut the fabric.

1 Taking your tambour hook and holder, chain stitch around the edge of the petal just inside the outline.

2 Then go over that line, still using the chain stitch, in a zigzag, placing each stitch on alternate sides of the original line. Try to keep your stitches as small as possible so the fabric will not fray. Once complete, cut out the petal very close to the chain stitches.

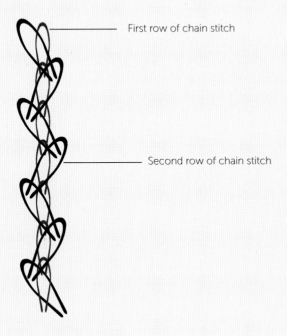

First row of chain stitch

Second row of chain stitch

HEMMING PETALS (OPTION 2)

The second option will give a much softer edge to your petals.

1 To use this method you need to cut out each individual petal piece with an additional 1cm (½in) seam allowance left around the edge, depending on the size of your petal. Ⓐ

2 Once you have cut these out you will need to hem the edges. Starting from one of the bottom edges, fold back half of the 1cm (½in) seam allowance, then fold it again. The raw edge will be hidden inside and the seam allowance folded to the back of the petal. It is sometimes difficult to manipulate the fold around the corners, so you will need to continuously fold the hem over itself. This will also create volume in the petal, allowing it to sit away from the fabric. Ⓑ

3 As you are folding the hem back you will need to stitch it in place as you go. Taking a small needle and single thread, put a small knot in the end of the thread and take your needle inside the folded seam allowance, hiding the knot.

4 Work around the petal, catching the back of the petal and then the folded seam allowance. Try not to catch too much of the back of the petal otherwise your stitches will show on the front. Ⓒ

◀ Designed by Renée Lindell and embroidered by Hand & Lock, these 3D flowers are hemmed as described in option 2.

Ⓐ

Ⓑ

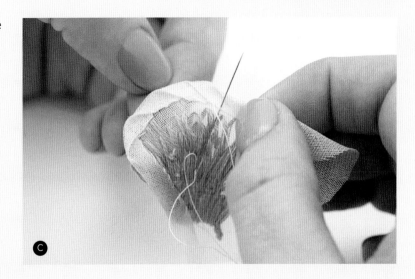

Ⓒ

STYLE 2

This style is a much more simplified version of the first style; it is versatile in terms of size, shape and visual appearance.

Again, you will need two types of fabric. The base fabric can be any type of fabric of your choosing; netting will be fine for this style. The flower fabric can be the same fabric as your base or a different one, I would suggest not using something too heavy as, again it will fall flat against the fabric. You may also want to use a variety of fabrics for the flowers as you can layer the fabrics or cluster different fabric flowers together.

Other equipment required includes an iron; scissors, Bondaweb, small needle (size 10 or 12), multi-purpose thread, pounce powder and tracing paper. You may also need Anchor Stranded Cotton, bugle beads and seed beads.

1 Depending on what type of fabric you have chosen for your flowers you will need to ensure that when these are cut to shape they do not fray. If you are using netting you will not have to follow the next few steps as netting does not fray.

2 Taking the flower fabric, cut into two pieces of equal size. Place each side back to back with a layer of Bondaweb inside, then iron together.

3 Make sure that you have ironed the two pieces of fabric together all over; you will be cutting the fabric, so if it has not bonded together all the way through the layers will separate. **A**

A

B

4 Design a flower shape no bigger than 5cm (2in) across; prick and pounce this onto your double-sided flower fabric, then cut out these flowers. **B**

5 Taking your base fabric, frame this up into a hoop or slate frame (see Setting up your frame, pages 44–48); you can now attach the flowers onto the fabric. There are many different ways of doing this, similar to the style above. You can use a large bead, French knots or upright bugle beads. To secure the flower to the base fabric initially, use a small cross stitch in the centre, which can then be covered with your chosen central decoration. **C**

6 As mentioned above, you can layer the flowers on top of one another to create height and texture. The first flower will need to be secured, as before, with a small cross stitch onto the base fabric; you can then continue to build up any number of desired layers. Once you have placed the top layer you can finish this with added central decoration (see page 139). **D**

TIP

You may want your flowers to sit with slightly more relief from the base fabric. To do this, stitch a circle of beads on the base fabric (the larger the beads the higher flower petals will sit) then place the centre of the flower into the centre of the circle. You can then stitch the centre down in your desired technique.

3D BEADING

Here is one technique that I use in combination with the 3D flowers but also to fill areas by placing the beads tightly against each other. Keep in mind the weight that the beads will create on your garment if you are using a large amount in one area.

UPSTANDING BUGLE BEADS

As mentioned for both styles of 3D flowers, you can use this technique together with others or by itself to create a different height to the base fabric.

You will need a needle (size 10 or 12), multi-purpose thread, bugle beads and seed beads.

1   Bring your needle up at the point where you would like your bugle bead to stand upright.

2   Thread one bugle bead onto the needle and thread and push down to the base fabric, 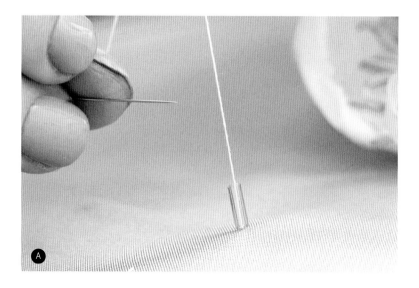 then thread a seed bead onto the needle and thread; do not push this all the way down to the top of the bugle bead.

3   Take your needle and thread back down the top of the bugle bead and back through to the back of the fabric. **B** Your seed bead acts like a stopper.

4   Pull the thread from the back; this will pull the seed bead down to sit neatly on the top of the bugle bead. **C**

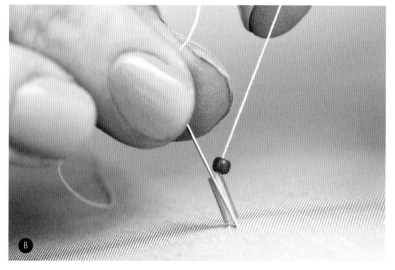

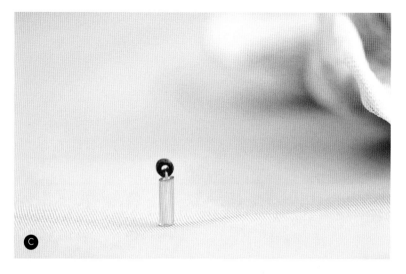

▶ Prada (Spring/Summer, 2016). This dress is covered in large sequins, sewn at one side to allow flexibility with movement. 3D bugle beads are used in the centre of the large green sequins.

MOVING ON

Embroidery is open to interpretation. As I have mentioned in throughout this book, there are many variations of traditional techniques. The techniques I have written about are in a style that I have developed for myself; others will have variations on the techniques I have written about, so don't be afraid to try different methods. It is good to feel comfortable with the way you execute your embroidery, and as long as you can you can achieve the same outcome, that is ok.

Throughout my career I have accumulated embroidery knowledge from my working life at Hand & Lock. However, there are many fashion designers and companies out there who are constantly influencing and defining new rules for embroidery in fashion. Hopefully the following will give you an idea as to who to look out for.

COMPANIES

HAND & LOCK: Traced back to 1767, Hand & Lock has embroidered for all the notable fashion house such as Christian Dior, Norman Hartnell and Hardy Amies, Burberry, Mary Katrantzou and Givenchy, as well as also serving emerging designers, interior designers, the Royal Forces and the Royal Family, costume designers for theatre, film, and television. It is truly an inspiring and influential company in the embroidery and fashion world.

MAISON LESAGE: Based in Paris, Maison Lesage has served not only the couturiers in Paris for almost 100 years but also fashion houses all over the world. Founded by Albert and Marie-Louise Lesage they attracted the attention of Elsa Schiaparelli, who stayed a faithful customer for 44 years. Now owned by Chanel, Maison Lesage still makes embroidery of the highest quality.

INFLUENCERS

JAMES MERRY: James Merry is a hand embroidery artist whose unique ideas have become widely recognised. He has made embroidery 'cool' for the younger generation with his sportswear series, while also working with Bjork to create innovative and eye-catching headdresses. James merry certainly knows how to push the boundaries of embroidery.

MARIE SOPHIE LOCKHART: Based in the USA but originally from Paris, Marie Sophie Lockhart, also know as Lockhart embroidery, is at the cutting edge of contemporary stitching. Marie uses simple hand embroidery on denim to create stylized and incredibly nonchalant pieces for all the big names in the music and fashion world. She considers Marc Jacobs, Stella McCartney and Christian Dior as clients and has created garments for Drake, Beyoncé and Miley Cyrus.

ITCHY SCRATCHY PATCHY: Itchy Scratchy Patchy was launched in 2015 by Christabel MacGreevy and Edie Campbell with a range of embroidered iron-on patches, inspired by British stereotypes and tabloid culture. The label has since grown to include finished garments, all of which are embroidered, embellished or printed with the same tongue-in-cheek individuality. The starting point was customization – the idea of taking control of ones clothes and having fun with them. There is a lightness and eccentricity to the spirit of the clothes.

NGUYEN CONG TRI: Personally, one of my favourite newcomers to the embroidery and fashion scene, Nguyen was first recognized in 2000 when he won 1st prize in the 'New Idea' category at Vietnam's Grand Prix. Based in Ho Chi Minh City, he continues to produce pioneering pieces that use a combination of incredibly detailed hand embroidery and beautifully crafted garments (shown right).

INDEX

ABOUT THE AUTHOR

Since graduating from Royal Central School of Speech and Drama with a degree in Costume Construction, Jessica has been at embroidery house Hand & Lock, working her way up from Design Assistant to Production Director. She is the youngest Production Director in the history of the company.

Jessica enjoys complex embroidery projects involving multiple techniques and a global army of embroiders. Her favourite projects have included embroidering an M16 assault rifle for the Peace One Day Project; a private commission for artists Gilbert & George; Mary Katrantzou (Autumn/Winter, 2014); and Burberry (Spring/Summer, 2016). She has also worked with a number of other fashion designers, including Louis Vuitton, Mulberry, Victoria Beckham, Aspinal of London and Adidas.

Since becoming a Director at Hand & Lock in 2014, Jessica has expanded the embroidery school with the introduction of classes all year round, introduced the annual Festival of Embroidery and transformed the Hand & Lock Prize for Embroidery into a world-class couture competition.

PICTURE CREDITS

All photography by Jutta Klee, except the following: Hand & Lock: pages 15 right, 19 bottom right, 21 right, 22, 24, 27 top, 27 bottom, 69, 78, 101, 123 and 134. Indigital: pages 5, 9 bottom, 16, 21 left, 50, 58, 66, 76 and 105. Mary Evans Picture Library: pages 14 and 17. Nguyen Cong Tri: pages 20, 130, 131 left, 131 right and 141. Ralph and Russo: pages 26, 37, 68, 79 and 81. Shutterstock: pages 2, 8, 9 top, 10, 13 left, 13 right, 15 left, 19 left, 19 top right, 23, 25, 28, 29 left, 29 right, 30, 33, 53, 70 left, 70 right, 71 left, 71 right, 72, 102, 104, 106, 107 left, 107 centre, 107 right, 126, 129 and 139. Illustrations pages 4, 6, 58 and 105 by Stephen Sheldon. Diagrams pages 38, 39, 74, 125 and 134 by the author.

ACKNOWLEDGEMENTS

Special thanks to Hand & Lock and all the team – For everything I have learnt.
Thank you also to Steven Sheldon for the illustrations, Nguyen Cong Tri, Ralph & Russo, Jutta Klee, Eleanor Pile and everyone else who helped or gave me advice.